quiet time

One Year Daily Devotional for Children in Grades 3-4

Quiet Time

One year daily devotional for children in grades 3-4

Published by Word of Life Local Church Ministries
A division of Word of Life Fellowship, Inc.
Joe Jordan - Executive Director
Don Lough - Director
Jack Wyrtzen & Harry Bollback - Founders
Ric Garland - VP of Local Church Ministries

> USA
> P.O. Box 600
> Schroon Lake, NY 12870
> 1-888-932-5827
> talk@wol.org
>
> Canada
> RR#8/Owen Sound
> ON, Canada N4K 5W4
> 1-800-461-3503 or (519) 376-3516
> lcm@wol.ca
>
> Web Address: www.wol.org

Publisher's Acknowledgements
Writers and Contributors: Sue Armbrecht, Jeanie Brown, Kris Paris, ChrisAnne Shultz, Bonnie Wertz
Editor: Sue Armbrecht
Curriculum Manager: Tim Filler
Cover Design and Layout: Sally Robison

Copyright © 2010 All rights reserved. Published by Word of Life Local Church Ministries. A division of Word of Life Fellowship, Inc. The purpose of Word of Life Fellowship worldwide is the evangelization and discipleship of youth through various means consistent with the Holy Scriptures to strengthen the church of Jesus Christ. No portion of this publication may be reproduced in any form without prior written permission of the publisher.

ISBN – 978-1-93547508-8
Printed in the United States of America

GOD loves you and wants to spend time with you!

Quiet Time is a special time that you set aside each day to read God's Word to get to know Him better and to learn how He wants you to live. During this time, God speaks to you through His Holy Word the Bible and you speak to God through prayer. What an adventure! As a Christian, spending this time everyday is very important for you to grow closer to God.

This **Quiet Time** will help you have a special time each day with the Lord. This booklet is divided into two sections. A Personal Prayer Diary section where you can write prayer requests to remind yourself to pray for people that you care about and things that are happening. The second section is the Quiet Time Activity Pages. Activities are written from the Bible verses for each day of the year to challenge you to understand the truths from God's Word.

All Word of Life **Quiet Times** use the same Scriptures for the week. This makes it easier for your whole family to discuss the passages together.

A NOTE TO PARENTS

This Quiet Time is a great opportunity for you to have fun together with your child. Here are some tips to help your child with their Quiet Time.

- Gather supplies needed for activities.
- Sit down at a prescribed time each day.
- Use the Bible to look up references together.
- Talk through the activity and personal application.
- Complete the week by documenting how many days were completed and writing an encouraging note.

YOUR DAILY QUIET TIME

Week 7 — Samuel's Story

Instead of going to preschool, Samuel's parents took him to Shiloh to live and be taught by the priest Eli.

Read the special Did You Know thoughts each week to learn something new!

SUNDAY — 1 Samuel 1:4-11,18

Hannah's Cry for Help

What was the one thing Hannah really wanted?
_____

What did she do in verse 10?
_____

What two things did she promise the Lord if He would give her a son? (v. 11).
1. _____
2. _____

According to verse 18, how did Hannah feel when she left?
_____

GET STARTED! What is the one thing you really want? _____
Have you prayed and asked God for it? Do it today!

Each day, read the Daily Scripture Passage.

MONDAY — 1 Samuel 1:20-28

Circle the answer God gave to Hannah's prayer on the light.

NO / WAIT / YES

GET STARTED! God always answers your prayers in one of these ways. Write one way God has answered one of your prayers.
_____

TUESDAY — 1 Samuel

Finish the statements.
1. Samuel was afraid to tell his vision from the Lord. (v. 15)
2. Everyone in Israel saw that Samuel was a _____ of the Lord.
3. The Lord continued to appear to _____ in Shiloh.

GET STARTED! Samuel listened to God. What grade would you give yourself for how you listen to God? _____

Complete the activity for the day and Take Action (in the red color) section to apply what you learned to your life!

Write down your prayer requests in your diary and spend time talking to God in prayer.

28

My Bible  | **My Quiet Time**  | **Crayons or Markers**  | **A Quiet Place**

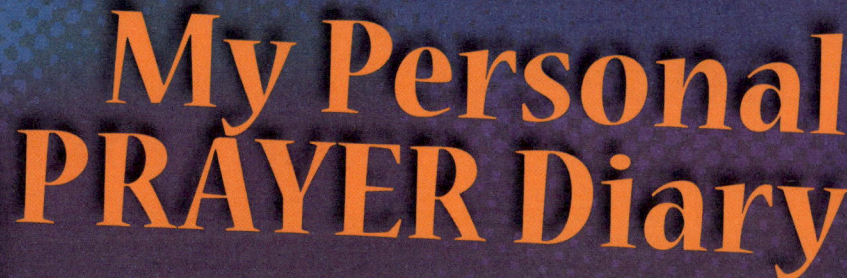

My Personal PRAYER Diary

Spending time with God in Prayer

Keeping a Personal Prayer Diary is a great way to remind yourself to pray for specific people and things. It also reminds you to thank God and to tell others when He answers your prayers. Your prayer time should include praying for friends and family. Especially pray for those who don't know Christ as their Savior. You should also pray for your Christian friends, your relatives and yourself. Pray that you will grow in your Christian life and become what God wants you to be. Get to know missionaries who serve the Lord in your area or around the world. Ask them for specific prayer requests. Write these on your prayer pages. Much of your prayer time should be used thanking and praising God. Tell God that you are thankful for your salvation, parents, home, friends, and answers to prayers. You should praise God for His beautiful creation, His holiness and His greatness. Some prayer time should include asking God to meet needs such as clothing, food or maybe a job for your dad. Maybe you could ask God to help you be more obedient. You must be careful not to be selfish and ask for things that you want only for you. As you are obedient to God, He will care for your needs.

Daily PRAYER Requests

Daily Prayer Requests are those things that you pray for each day. Maybe someone in your family will be traveling one day and you ask God to protect them as they travel. For each request, write the date that you started praying for it and how God answered your prayer.

NAME	DATE	HOW MY PRAYER WAS ANSWERED

Daily PRAYER Requests

NAME	DATE	HOW MY PRAYER WAS ANSWERED

Daily PRAYER Requests

NAME	DATE	HOW MY PRAYER WAS ANSWERED
....	⬤	_____
....	⬤	_____
....	⬤	_____
....	⬤	_____
....	⬤	_____
....	⬤	_____
....	⬤	_____
....	⬤	_____
....	⬤	_____
....	⬤	_____
....	⬤	_____
....	⬤	_____
....	⬤	_____
....	⬤	_____

Daily PRAYER Requests

NAME	DATE	HOW MY PRAYER WAS ANSWERED
....	○	_____
....	○	_____
....	○	_____
....	○	_____
....	○	_____
....	○	_____
....	○	_____
....	○	_____
....	○	_____
....	○	_____
....	○	_____
....	○	_____
....	○	_____
....	○	_____

The Weekly Prayer Request Chart can be used to remind you to pray for specific requests either once a week or more often. Write down the names of friends and family members. Don't forget to include those that need to be saved. Put the names of your church leaders and missionaries that you know so that you can remember to pray for them as well. For each request, write the date that you started praying and how God answered your prayer.

Weekly PRAYER Requests

SUNDAY - Family & Friends

NAME — **DATE** — **HOW MY PRAYER WAS ANSWERED**

Missionaries & Church Leaders

I thank GOD for...   I praise GOD for...

Weekly PRAYER Requests

MONDAY – Family & Friends

NAME	DATE	HOW MY PRAYER WAS ANSWERED
....	⬤	_____
....	⬤	_____
....	⬤	_____
....	⬤	_____
....	⬤	_____

Missionaries & Church Leaders

....	⬤	_____
....	⬤	_____
....	⬤	_____
....	⬤	_____

I thank GOD for . . .   I praise GOD for . . .

_____

_____

Weekly PRAYER Requests

TUESDAY – Family & Friends

NAME	DATE	HOW MY PRAYER WAS ANSWERED
....		_____
....		_____
....		_____
....		_____
....		_____

Missionaries & Church Leaders

NAME	DATE	HOW MY PRAYER WAS ANSWERED
....		_____
....		_____
....		_____
....		_____

I thank GOD for . . .   I praise GOD for . . .

_____

_____

Weekly PRAYER Requests

WEDNESDAY – Family & Friends

NAME	DATE	HOW MY PRAYER WAS ANSWERED
....		_____
....		_____
....		_____
....		_____
....		_____

Missionaries & Church Leaders

NAME	DATE	HOW MY PRAYER WAS ANSWERED
....		_____
....		_____
....		_____
....		_____

I thank GOD for... I praise GOD for...

_____
_____

Weekly PRAYER Requests

THURSDAY – Family & Friends

NAME	DATE	HOW MY PRAYER WAS ANSWERED
....		_____
....		_____
....		_____
....		_____
....		_____

Missionaries & Church Leaders

....		_____
....		_____
....		_____
....		_____

I thank GOD for . . .   I praise GOD for . . .

_____

_____

Weekly PRAYER Requests

FRIDAY – Family & Friends

NAME	DATE	HOW MY PRAYER WAS ANSWERED
....	⬤	_____
....	⬤	_____
....	⬤	_____
....	⬤	_____
....	⬤	_____

Missionaries & Church Leaders

....	⬤	_____
....	⬤	_____
....	⬤	_____
....	⬤	_____

I thank GOD for... I praise GOD for...

_____

_____

_____

Weekly PRAYER Requests

SATURDAY – Family & Friends

NAME	DATE	HOW MY PRAYER WAS ANSWERED
....		_____
....		_____
....		_____
....		_____
....		_____

Missionaries & Church Leaders

NAME	DATE	HOW MY PRAYER WAS ANSWERED
....		_____
....		_____
....		_____
....		_____

I thank GOD for … I praise GOD for …

_____

_____

Week 1 — Let's Start From the Beginning

The shortest chapter of the Bible also happens to be the exact middle of the Bible. It is Psalm 117.

SUNDAY
Psalm 104:1-9

TRAIN YOUR BRAIN — God is the Creator of the heavens and the earth. Color the picture.

GET STARTED! — Some people and books tell you that the earth came about by evolution. Share what you have learned today about God creating the earth with your teacher or a friend.

MONDAY
Psalm 104:14-19

TRAIN YOUR BRAIN — The earth was made to meet the needs of all of God's creation. Match each of God's creations to its purpose.

Grass	Places for birds to nest
Oil	To tell the seasons
High hills or mountains	Home for the wild goats
Trees	Makes a man's face shine (glisten)
Moon	For the cattle

GET STARTED! — What are your favorite parts of God's creation?
Your favorite animal _____
part of nature _____
food _____.
Thank God for His beautiful works!

TUESDAY
Psalm 104:27-31

TRAIN YOUR BRAIN — God takes care of all your needs. Find the hidden pictures of the following needs God provides for you: food, water, clothes, and a home.

GET STARTED! — How can you thank God for all He has done for you? You can tell Him in your prayers or by singing a song of praise to Him. Choose one to do right now.

16

WEDNESDAY
Psalm 105:5-12

Train Your Brain

God keeps all of His promises. Fill in the letters of the names of the people who received promises from God.

1. _ B _ _ _ _ _ _ v.9   2. _ _ A _ _ v.9
3. _ _ _ _ B v.10

Get Started! God's Word tells us that it is better to not make a promise than to make a promise and break it. Did you keep all your promises this week? **YES   NO**

THURSDAY
Psalm 105:17-22

Train Your Brain

Place the colored letters in order from the story in the boxes below.

DO YOU REMEMBER THE STORY O**F** JOSEPH FROM THE BOOK OF GENESIS? HIS OWN BROTHERS SOLD JOSEPH INTO SL**A**VERY. NEXT, HIS OWN MASTER THREW HIM IN PR**I**SON. FINALLY, **T**HE KING RELEASED JOSEPH FROM PRISON AND BROUG**H**T HIM INTO THE PALACE TO MAKE HIM IN CHARGE O**F** THE KING'S HO**U**SE AND AL**L** HIS POSSESSIONS.

THROUGHOUT HIS LIFE, JOSEPH REMAINED
☐ ☐ ☐ ☐ ☐ ☐ ☐ ☐
TO THE LORD.

Get Started! Joseph was always faithful and obedient to the Lord no matter what kind of day he was having. Circle the kind of day that you are having. **Good   Bad** Even if you are having a bad day, are you still being faithful to God and trusting Him?

FRIDAY
Psalm 105:26-27

God chose Moses and Aaron to lead His people out of Egypt. Help Moses and Aaron get through the maze and out of Egypt.

EGYPT

PROMISED LAND

Get Started! A faithful person doesn't quit. Finish this sentence. "I will be faithful to God in _____."

SATURDAY
Psalm 105:31-45

Train Your Brain

How did God meet the needs of the Israelites? Answer the questions below.

Verse 37 What did the Israelites take with them when they left? _____
Verse 39 God covered them with a _____ and gave them _____ for light at night.
Verse 40 God gave them what two kinds of food? _____ _____
Verse 41 What came out of the rock? _____

Get Started! There is a difference between **NEEDS** and **WANTS**.
Write a *need* that you have. _____
Write a *want* that you have. _____
Do you complain if you don't get something you want?
Be sure to thank God for taking care of your needs.

---

comment corner WE'RE PROUD OF YOU stay with it KEEP TRYING BE FAITHFUL you can do it YOU ARE SPECIAL keep going KEEP IT UP GOD LOVES YOU!

Days Completed

Parent or Leader, circle a comment and/or write your own.

Week 2

God Protects and Provides

Are you a complainer? During the time of Moses, God punished two complainers, Dathan and Abiram, by causing the earth to open up under them. The men and everything they owned disappeared into the earth.

SUNDAY
Psalm 106:7-15

List three things God did for the Israelites from verses 9, 10, and 11.

Verse 9 _____

Verse 10 _____

Verse 11 _____

MONDAY
Psalm 106:16-25

Write TRUE or FALSE

_____ The earth opened and swallowed Dathan and Abiram. (v. 17)

_____ They made a pig statue in Horeb and worshipped it. (v. 19)

_____ They praised God for all the great things that He had done for them in Egypt. (v. 21)

_____ They believed God's Word. (v. 24)

_____ They did not listen to the voice of the Lord. (v. 25)

Circle the answer that applies to you. I complain

SOMETIMES   NEVER   OFTEN

Share with a leader, Sunday school teacher, or friend how God has protected you.

TUESDAY
Psalm 106:44-48

Decode the message below by selecting the letter in the alphabet that comes after the letter. For example: R=S, Z=A, N=O.

F N C   R G N V D C

K N U D

Z M C   L D Q B X

S N   S G D

B G H K C Q D M   N E

H R Q Z D K

Just as God cares about us, we need to care about others. Write or send an e-mail message to a college student encouraging him or her to be faithful in reading God's Word.

WEDNESDAY
Psalm 107:10-16

 Unscramble the letters to find out how God helped His people.

Verse 13 He **VSADE** _____ them out of their distresses or trouble.

Verse 14 He **GUROBHT** _____ them out of darkness.

 Think of a time when you were in trouble and God helped you through it. Share that memory with your parents. Ask your parents how God has helped them when they were in trouble.

THURSDAY
Psalm 107:28-32

Help the fishermen to get out of the storm and into safety.

FRIDAY
Psalm 107:33-38

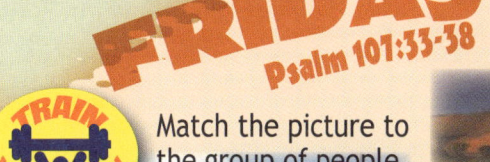 Match the picture to the group of people.

Wicked People   Hungry (needy) People

 Are you afraid of storms?
YES   NO
What kind of storm scares you?
_____
Who protects you through the storm?
_____

 Do you think of yourself as a wise person? YES NO Write down one thing you have learned about God this week.
_____
_____

SATURDAY
Psalm 108:1-6, 12, 13

 Whom did David count on to defeat his enemies? Color in the letters of the answer.

Write down two words from verse 4 that David uses to describe God.

1. _____

2. _____

 Even today, the nation Israel has many enemies. Ask a parent or leader to tell you the name of a nation that is an enemy of Israel. Write it here. _____

Pray for the people of Israel and their enemies to come to know Jesus as their Savior.

---

comment corner — WE'RE PROUD OF YOU · stay with it · KEEP TRYING · BE FAITHFUL · you can do it · YOU ARE SPECIAL · keep going · KEEP IT UP · GOD LOVES YOU!

Days Completed

Parent or Leader, circle a comment and/or write your own.

Week 3
Fearing the Lord Is the Healthy Choice

In Psalm 109:2, David says that some people lied about him. His three worst enemies were King Saul; Shimei, a member of Saul's family; and his own son, Absalom.

SUNDAY
Psalm 109:1-5

 David was wrongfully accused, lied about, and rumors were spread about him. What does David do? Write the answer on the line. It is found at the end of verse 4.

_____

 Write down the first initials of two people who may have wrongfully blamed you, lied about you, or spoken to you in a very mean way. Then, just as David did, pray for them each day this week.

_____

_____

MONDAY
Psalm 109:16-20

 David prayed for God to deal with a wicked man. Circle the wicked ways of the man that David describes in verses 16-18.

- He helps people.
- He is known for cursing people.
- He persecuted (hurt) needy people.
- He gave to the poor.
- He is known for talking kindly.

 If you or someone you know has a problem with a bully, talk to your parents or your leader.

TUESDAY
Psalm 109:21-29

 If the word(s) describes David, write D in the box. If the word(s) describes the enemy, write E in the box.

☐ Needy
☐ Shame
☐ Arise (Attack)
☐ Weak knees
☐ Wounded heart
☐ Curse

 Verse 21 is a great verse to underline in your Bible for you to read when you have a problem.

WEDNESDAY
Psalm 110:1-7

Psalm 110:1 is the most quoted psalm verse in the New Testament. Jesus sits at the right hand of God. One day every person in every country will worship Jesus.

One day Jesus will be the leader of every country in the world. Ask your parent or a leader to pray with you for your country's leaders today.

On the map put stars on the places that you will pray for.

THURSDAY
Psalm 111:2-10

The fear of the Lord means *respecting God because of who He is*. Write out the first sentence from verse 10.

_____

_____

One way that you can fear the Lord is to obey your parents. The next time a parent asks you to do something, obey right away.

FRIDAY
Psalm 112:1-10

Find the blessings in the puzzle that a person receives by *fearing the Lord*:

COMPASSION									
FEARLESS	U	R	W	F	N	S	C	D	L	S
GRACIOUS	F	A	E	D	O	U	A	S	V	A
RIGHTEOUS	G	R	A	C	I	O	U	S	U	F
WEALTH	W	M	L	I	S	E	I	E	M	T
	H	H	T	J	S	T	Z	L	E	B
	A	T	H	C	A	H	Z	R	J	F
	H	V	U	M	P	G	J	A	K	B
	B	L	V	Y	M	I	W	E	S	F
	S	E	D	A	O	R	B	F	Z	P
	I	F	N	B	C	U	L	G	C	H

Write down one way you will be a blessing to someone else this week.

_____

SATURDAY
Psalm 113:1-9

Fill in the missing letters.

___raise the Lord!

From the ___ising of the sun.

The Lord is high (exalted) above all ___ations.

He raises the poor from the ___ust.

As a joyful (happy) ___other of children.

Ask your parents what you can do to help the poor and needy.

Days Completed

comment corner — WE'RE PROUD OF YOU • stay with it • KEEP TRYING • BE FAITHFUL • you can do it • YOU ARE SPECIAL • keep going • KEEP IT UP • GOD LOVES YOU!

Parent or Leader, circle a comment and/or write your own.

Week 4
Corinthian Comforters Created by Christ

Ancient people had many uses for clay jars. A potter could dry his pottery in the sun or in a kiln. Only pottery dried in kilns were able to hold water.

SUNDAY
2 Corinthians 5:1-10

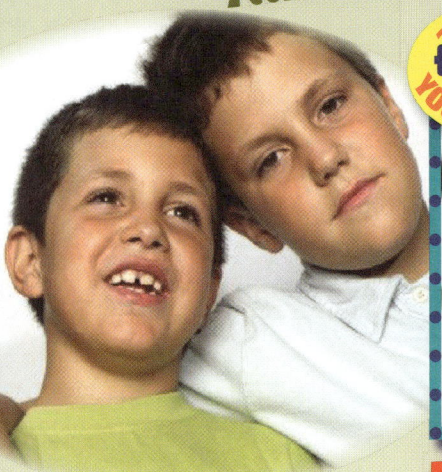

Color in the dotted areas to find the word that fills in the blanks.

God will __ __ __ __ __ __ __ you when you are sick or sad. Do you know someone who is sick or sad? Comfort that person by visiting or sending a card this week.

MONDAY
2 Corinthians 5:1-10

In verse 22 we read that God has sealed those who have put their faith and trust in Him. This means He placed His seal of ownership on them. If you have accepted Christ as your Savior, draw or put a picture of yourself on the seal.

Ask your parents to tell you at least one way they see you act as a Christian.

TUESDAY
2 Corinthians 5:1-10

Unscramble the words from the verses which talk about forgiveness. The first letter is given.

cfodnicnee (v. 3)
C _____

rtahe (v. 4)
H _____

rtsae (v. 4)
T _____

egrfovi (v. 7)
F _____

trmocfo (v. 7)
C _____

tnbedeio (v. 9)
O _____

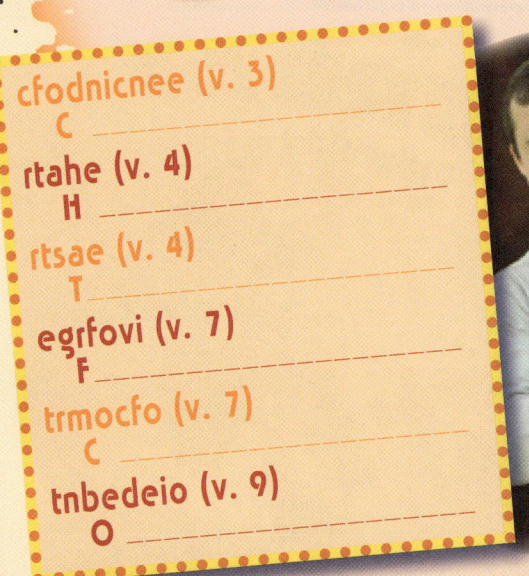

In verses 5-9, you are taught to forgive. Is there someone you need to forgive? Do it today!

WEDNESDAY
2 Corinthians 2:14-16; 3:2-3

What is your favorite smell? Flowers? Pizza? Verse 15 talks about how your actions around others are like good smells or bad smells.

GET STARTED! Are your actions a sweet smell or do your actions stink? Circle the flower or skunk for your answer. If your life shows others that you are trying to live God's way, write your name on the heart. Be a good example this week.

THURSDAY
2 Corinthians 3:17

Verse 17 tells us that where the spirit of the Lord is, there is what? _____

Write down one of the freedoms (liberties) that you have.

Draw and color the flag of your country.

GET STARTED! Your armed forces fight for your freedoms. Pray for the men and women serving in the armed forces from your church. Ask God to protect them.

FRIDAY
2 Corinthians 4:4-6

Have you ever tried to play a game wearing a blindfold? The god of this world (age) is Satan, and he likes to blind the hearts of unsaved people. What is Satan trying to keep people from seeing or understanding? Color the X's to find the answer.

```
XTXHXXEXXLXXIXGXXHXXTX
XXXOXXFXXXTXXXHXXXEXX
XGXXXOXXXSXXXXPXEXXXLXX
```

 God's power can help give you courage to share the Gospel with someone else. Who will you tell about Jesus this week? _____

SATURDAY
2 Corinthians 4:16-18

Your body will wear out someday. Circle the things listed below that will make you stronger in Christ.

- Fight with my brother
- Read the Bible
- Pray
- Do my Quiet Time
- Watch TV
- Ride my bike
- Share my testimony
- Go to Olympians
- Memorize Scripture verses

 Did you do a Quiet Time last year? _____
Are you trying to be faithful this year? _____
Write down the number of days you completed your Quiet Time this week in the box below.

Days Completed

comment corner — WE'RE PROUD OF YOU • stay with it • KEEP TRYING • BE FAITHFUL • you can do it • YOU ARE SPECIAL • keep going • KEEP IT UP • GOD LOVES YOU!

Parent or Leader, circle a comment and/or write your own.

Week 5 — Living a Life That Is Right On

Paul and Barnabas collected money to take to the Christians in Jerusalem who suffered through two earthquakes and a famine.

SUNDAY
2 Corinthians 5:7-10

Have you ever been in a courtroom?
Who makes the final decision? _____ Someday, all Christians will stand before Christ, and He will judge our works (v. 10). He will give us rewards based on our good works for Him.

GET STARTED! Circle the works that will please God.

- Giving money to missionaries because your parents made you do it.
- **Giving money to missionaries because you want to reach others with the Gospel.**
- Obeying your parents so you will not get punished.
- **Obeying your parents because it is right.**

MONDAY
2 Corinthians 5:16-17

According to verse 17, when someone accepts Christ as Savior, they become a new

_____.

Use a yellow crayon or marker to color the letters of the word (v. 17).

CPRMEFAVTSUIROEN

GET STARTED! Finish the sentence.
As an unsaved person, I may want to

_____;

but as a Christian, I should

_____ instead.

TUESDAY
2 Corinthians 6:2-10

Circle the six words from this passage that tell us about Paul's ministry.

REJOICING
UNKNOWN
SALVATION
MINISTRY
SORROWFUL
PATIENCE

```
S A L V A T I O N P
O U N K N O W N Y A
I M I N I S T R Y T
T L C X X N G W B I
A Z I C K T C N N E
V K O U Z J Q E F N
L S J R R O W F U C
R E J O I C I N G E
S O R R O W F U L U
```

GET STARTED! Paul and his ministry friends went through a lot in order to bring the message of salvation to others. Is it hard for you to talk to others? YES   NO

24

WEDNESDAY
2 Corinthians 6:14-17

Your choice of friends is very important. In Paul's first letter to the Corinthians (1 Corinthians 15:33), Paul warns that bad friends can ruin you. How do your friends influence you?

Friend wants you to:	What would you say to him
Watch a bad TV show	_____
Play a bad video game	_____
Smoke a cigarette	_____
Steal a candy bar	_____

GET STARTED! Write the name of a friend who helps you make right choices.
_____

THURSDAY
2 Corinthians 7:2-4

Connect the dots to find the answer to the following: The Corinthians were truly repentant (sorry) for their sins, and this filled Paul's heart with _____.

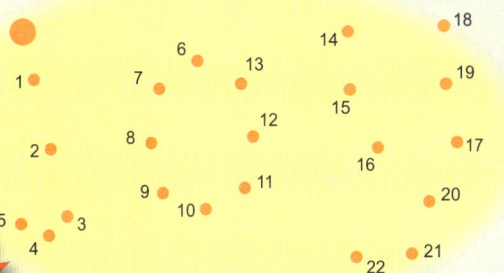

True repentance means having sincere sorrow over your sin which makes you want to change your ways and not repeat your sin.
Do you remember the last time you sinned? _____
Did you repent of that sin? _____

FRIDAY
2 Corinthians 8:1-4

Do you think that the Macedonian churches were rich? God expects all Christians to give. How can you give to help missions and the church? Fill in the missing vowels under each picture to form the word.

m__n__y   pr__y__ng   t__m__   t__l__nts

GET STARTED! Ask your leader about collecting some money in Olympians to meet the special needs of a missionary child.

SATURDAY
2 Corinthians 8:16-24

Money for the Lord's work should be used wisely. Paul tells the Corinthians how the offering was handled. To solve this puzzle, put the letter in the alphabet that follows the letter given. Example: for "S" put "T," for "Z" put "A." As Christians we must be what?

G N M D R S   H M   S G D   R H F G S

N E   F N C   Z M C   L D M.

GET STARTED! Pray and ask God to help you be honest in all you do.

Comment Corner — WE'RE PROUD OF YOU · stay with it · KEEP TRYING BE FAITHFUL · you can do it · YOU ARE SPECIAL · keep going · KEEP IT UP · GOD LOVES YOU!

Parent or Leader, circle a comment and/or write your own.

Days Completed

Week 6 — Christian Giving, Living, and Thinking

SUNDAY
2 Corinthians 9:6-8

A criminal could not be beaten with more than forty stripes (Deuteronomy 25:1-3). To avoid a miscount, the number of stripes given was thirty-nine. Paul was beaten with thirty-nine stripes five different times.

Train Your Brain

If you were a farmer and wanted to have a large crop, would you plant **a few seeds** or **lots of seeds?** That was a pretty easy question, right?

Now apply that lesson to your giving. It is not just about **how much** you give, but it is also about the way in which you give your gift. Finish the face to show what kind of giver God wants you to be.

Get Started! Really pray and think about what God would want you to give.

MONDAY
2 Corinthians 10:3-5

Train Your Brain

When your dog is on his leash, he is your captive. You control him. As a Christian, we need to take every _____ captive. Shade in the O's to find the correct answer to fill in the blank.

```
XXXXXXXXXXXXXXXXXXXXXXXXXXXXXXXXXX
XOOOOOXOXXOXOOOOOXOXXOXOOOOXOXXOXOOOOOX
XOXXXOXOXXOXOXXXXXOXXOXOXXXXOXOXOX
XOXXXOXOXXOXOXXXXXOXOXOXOXXXOOOXOX
XOOOOOXOXXOXOXXXXXOOXOXOOOOXOXOOXOX
XOXXXXXOXXOXOXXXXXOXOOXOXXXXXOXXXOX
XOXXXXXOOOOXOOOOOXOXXOXOOOOXOXXXOX
XXXXXXXXXXXXXXXXXXXXXXXXXXXXXXXXXX
```

Get Started! Write the name of your favorite book: _____;
TV show _____;
computer or video game _____.
Circle the ones that help you to think right.

TUESDAY
2 Corinthians 11:3-4, 13-15

Train Your Brain

Satan comes in many different ways to try to trick us. In these verses, he is described as a
_____ (v. 3) and an
_____ (v. 14).
He uses false _____ (v. 13) --- people who don't teach the truth about Jesus.

"The Bible says....but in my opinion..."

Get Started! Finish the sentence. Satan may want me to _____, but God says _____.

WEDNESDAY
2 Corinthians 11:24-28

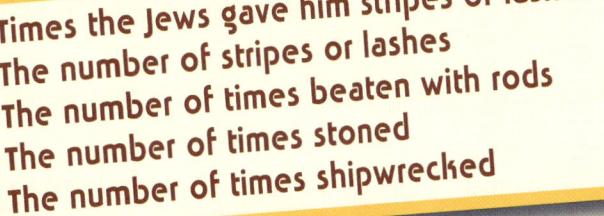

Draw a line from the treatment Paul received to the number of times it happened.

Times the Jews gave him stripes or lashes	3
The number of stripes or lashes	5
The number of times beaten with rods	1
The number of times stoned	39
The number of times shipwrecked	3

Ask a parent or leader to tell you the name of a missionary who is serving Christ in a dangerous place. Write the missionary's name in your prayer diary, and pray for that missionary this week.

THURSDAY
2 Corinthians 12:7-10

Paul had some kind of problem (v. 7). He asked the Lord three times to take it away, but the Lord did not do so. Instead, solve the code to find out what the Lord said to Paul.

= A   = E   = I   = O   = U

"My gr♥c♪ △s s🌍ff△c△♪nt f🦟r you (thee)."

God may allow a Christian to suffer to bring glory to Himself. Write down the name of a godly Christian who is handicapped.

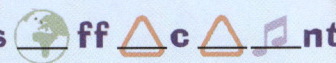 Pray for that person.

FRIDAY
2 Corinthians 12:11-18

Complete the crossword puzzle using the clues. The starting letter for each word is already given.

v.14 P
v.13 F
v.12 W
v.14 C
v.18 S
v.15 S
v.16 C
v.17 S
v.?? T

Paul served others without expecting anything in return. Ask to do a chore for a neighbor. Do not accept any money or treats for your work.

SATURDAY
2 Corinthians 13:5-8

When you go to a doctor, he examines you to see if you are healthy. How can you examine (or test) yourself to see that you are a Christian. Take the following true and false test.

____ 1. I know that I am a sinner.
____ 2. Jesus paid for my sins when He died on the cross.
____ 3. I know that Jesus rose from the dead.
____ 4. I am not good enough to get to heaven by myself (good works, my family...).
____ 5. I have asked Jesus to forgive me of my sins and come into my heart.

If you have answered True to all of the statements, you have passed the test.

If you didn't pass the test, or are not certain that you are saved, talk to a parent, teacher, or pastor.

---

comment corner — WE'RE PROUD OF YOU • stay with it • KEEP TRYING BE FAITHFUL • you can do it • YOU ARE SPECIAL • keep going • KEEP IT UP • GOD LOVES YOU!

Days Completed

Parent or Leader, circle a comment and/or write your own.

Week 7

Samuel's Story

Instead of going to preschool, Samuel's parents took him to Shiloh to live and be taught by the priest Eli.

SUNDAY
1 Samuel 1:4-11,18

Hannah's Cry for Help

What was the one thing Hannah really wanted?
_____

What did she do in verse 10?
_____

What two things did she promise the Lord if He would give her a son? (v. 11).
1. _____
2. _____

According to verse 18, how did Hannah feel when she left?
_____

GET STARTED!
What is the one thing you really want? _____
Have you prayed and asked God for it? Do it today!

MONDAY
1 Samuel 1:20-28

Circle the answer God gave to Hannah's prayer on the light.

GET STARTED!
God always answers your prayers in one of these ways. Write one way God has answered one of your prayers.
_____
_____

TUESDAY
1 Samuel 3:15-21

Finish the statements.

1. Samuel was afraid to tell _____ his vision from the Lord. (v. 15)
2. Everyone in Israel saw that Samuel was a _____ of the Lord. (v.20)
3. The Lord continued to appear to _____ in Shiloh.

GET STARTED!
Samuel listened to God. What grade would you give yourself for how you listen to God? _____

28

WEDNESDAY
1 Samuel 6:10-15

Israel

What happened to the Philistines when they stole the ark of the Lord from the people of Israel? God punished them with sores and mice. Now, they wanted to return the ark. Help the cows carrying the ark find their way back to Israel.

 **GET STARTED!**

Is it right to take something that does not belong to you? _____

If you have done that, you need to apologize and return the item to its owner.

THURSDAY
1 Samuel 7:1-6

The people of Israel thought of the ark as their good luck charm, but it was God who had really won their battles.

List some "good luck charms" people have today.

_____
_____
_____
_____

 **GET STARTED!**

Do you believe in luck or in God? Finish the sentence. I trust God to
_____
_____
_____

FRIDAY
1 Samuel 8:10-21

The people of Israel no longer recognized God as their King. They wanted a king like the other nations. Unscramble the words of what a king would take from them.

SSNO _____
IEFLDS _____
TRESDGHAU _____
TTENH _____
of their flocks (sheep)

GET STARTED!

God wants to be King of your life. Will you give your life completely to Him? If so, write GOD on the throne.

SATURDAY
1 Samuel 9:17-24

Answer the questions.

Who did God choose to be Israel's first king? _____ (v. 17)
Saul would save the people of Israel from whom? _____ (v. 16)
What tribe was Saul from? _____ (v. 21)
What part of the meat was given to Saul? _____ (v. 24 – this was the most honored part)

Must a person be popular or good-looking to be a godly Christian?

What are you trying to be? Circle one:

popular   godly

 **GET STARTED!**

comment corner

WE'RE PROUD OF YOU · stay with it · KEEP TRYING · BE FAITHFUL · you can do it · YOU ARE SPECIAL · keep going · KEEP IT UP · GOD LOVES YOU!

Parent or Leader, circle a comment and/or write your own.

Days Completed

29

Week 8

A Popular Man But a Poor King

Where did the people of Israel sharpen their tools? Since there were no blacksmiths in Israel, the farmers took all of their tools to their enemies, the Philistines, to be sharpened. (1 Samuel 13:20)

SUNDAY
1 Samuel 10:1-8, 17-19

Write "T" for true and "F" for false beside each statement.

_____ 1. Samuel poured oil over Saul's head to anoint him. (v. 1)
_____ 2. The donkeys he had been searching for were still lost. (v. 2)
_____ 3. Saul would be given three loaves of bread. (v. 4)
_____ 4. Samuel told Saul the Spirit of the Lord would come upon him. (v. 6)
_____ 5. By wanting a king, the people had rejected God. (v. 19)

Do you want to be part of the popular group at school? _____
Will being part of that group hurt your testimony as a Christian? _____

MONDAY
1 Samuel 12:13-23

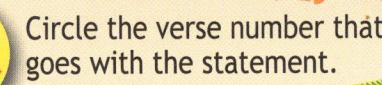

Circle the verse number that goes with the statement.

1. Samuel told the people not to rebel against the Lord's commands.   v.13   v.15
2. The Lord sent thunder and rain to the people.   v.16   v.18
3. The people realized that they made a mistake by asking for a king.   v.19   v.23

The Bible teaches that more people will choose *Man's Way over God's Way*. Circle the sign that shows the direction that you are choosing for your life right now.

TUESDAY
1 Samuel 13: 5-14

Because Saul was impatient, he disobeyed God and made a sacrifice before Samuel arrived. Circle the statements below that show obedience and "X" out the disobedient ones.

I'll do it later.

I'll do it right away.

Can I help you?

Yes, Mom.

Do it yourself.

Why doesn't she have to do it?

I would be glad to.

I don't want to.

Are you impatient sometimes? Yes   No
Does your impatience get you into trouble? Yes   No
Ask God to help you learn how to handle problems or people without becoming impatient.

WEDNESDAY
1 Samuel 15:1-11

Saul disobeyed again. Shade in all the O's to find out what the Lord had told Saul to do in this battle against the Amalekites.

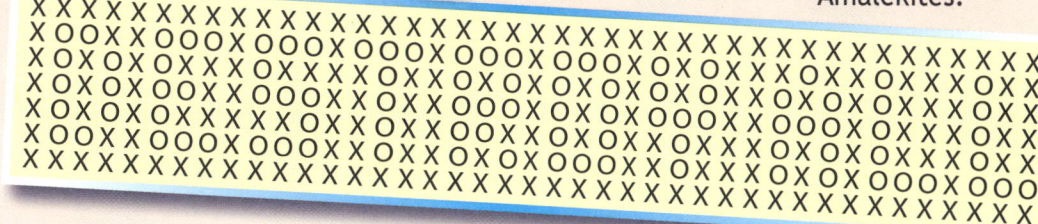

Get Started!

God wasn't pleased with Saul because he only *partly* obeyed God. Circle the word that describes how you finished the following:

1. Yesterday I obeyed my parents and teachers — partly / completely
2. Yesterday I did my chores — partly / completely
3. Yesterday I did my homework — partly / completely

THURSDAY
1 Samuel 15:13-26

Circle the correct answer.

1. What reason did Saul give Samuel for keeping some sheep?
   Sacrifice   Dinner
2. What consequence did Saul get for his disobedience?
   Pay a fine   Rejected as king

Get Started!

Obedience is serious business to God. Have you disobeyed today? Confess it right away.

FRIDAY
1 Samuel 16:1; 6-13

Write down ways your heart can be pleasing to God.

_____
_____
_____

Get Started!

Underline 1 Samuel 16:7 in your Bible. Are you happy with the way God made you? Are you more concerned about how you look or if your heart is pleasing God?

SATURDAY
1 Samuel 17:1-16

Find the eight words.

- Champion
- Philistines
- Servants
- David
- Goliath
- Helmet
- Spear
- Youngest

Get Started!

Goliath "bullied" the children of Israel. Do you know someone who is a bully? _____
Ask your parent to pray with you about how to treat a bully.

comment corner

WE'RE PROUD OF YOU • stay with it • KEEP TRYING • BE FAITHFUL • you can do it • YOU ARE SPECIAL • keep going • KEEP IT UP • GOD LOVES YOU!

Parent or Leader, circle a comment and/or write your own.

Days Completed

Week 9: The Giant Slayer and the Jealous King

Standing over nine feet tall, Goliath was a big dude! Would you believe his coat of armor weighed about 125 pounds?

SUNDAY
1 Samuel 17:20-25

TRAIN YOUR BRAIN

Goliath was not just challenging the armies of Israel; he was challenging God. Who was the enemy of God? Who was the friend of God? *The Philistines* or *the Israelites*? Write their names in the correct blanks.

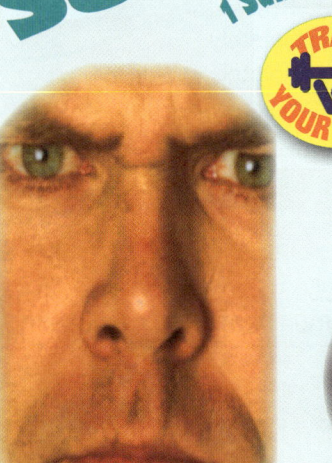

ENEMY
_____

FRIEND
_____

GET STARTED!

If you have never accepted Christ as your personal Savior, you are still an enemy of God. Write your name on the line that tells what you are to God.

MONDAY
1 Samuel 17:36-47

TRAIN YOUR BRAIN

Draw a line from the person to what they said.

GOLIATH	Your servant has killed both a lion and a bear.
DAVID	I'll give your flesh to the birds and the beasts of the field.
SAUL	Go, and may the Lord be with you.

GET STARTED!

What makes you afraid? _____
Try reading Psalm 56:3, which David wrote, to give you courage.

TUESDAY
1 Samuel 17:48-58

TRAIN YOUR BRAIN

David had the victory over Goliath because he fought in the name of the Lord. Solve the puzzle using the code.

GET STARTED!

Whatever happens to you this week, will you trust God as David did? **REMEMBER**, God is with you. **SAY** to God, "I will trust You." Then **DO** what He is giving you the courage to do.

WEDNESDAY
1 Samuel 18:1-16

Get Started! Saul was jealous of David. Cross out the ways God would *not* want you to be popular.

- By the clothes you wear
- By caring about others
- By acting better than others
- By acting godly
- By encouraging others
- By talking about others behind their back

Train Your Brain Circle the correct answer to the following questions.

1. David had a best friend. Who was it? (v. 3)
   Saul   Goliath   Jonathan
2. The women sang about David slaying how many? (v. 7)
   100   10,000   1,000
3. Saul was _____ of David. (v. 12)
   a friend   an enemy   afraid
4. Israel and Judah _____ David. (v. 16)
   loved   hated   mocked

THURSDAY
1 Samuel 19:1-12

Train Your Brain Draw a line from the name of the person to what they did in this passage.

Saul — let David down through a window
Michal — spoke well of David
David — fled and escaped death
Jonathan — tried to kill David

Get Started! Once again, Saul let his jealousy control him. Circle the ways that will help you overcome jealousy.

- Pray for the well-being of others
- Make fun of those people
- Be grateful for what God has done for you
- Thank God for that person.
- Get that person in trouble.

FRIDAY
1 Samuel 20:11-23

Train Your Brain What was Jonathan going to use to warn David? Connect the dots to find out.

Get Started! Do you have a best friend? _____
Would you warn your friend of any trouble? _____
Have you told your friend about Jesus? _____
Do it today.

SATURDAY
1 Samuel 20:30-42

 **Train Your Brain** Jealousy often turns into hate. Saul even tried to kill his son, Jonathan, because of David. Jonathan and David had to say "goodbye" to each other. Help David find his way out of the city.

 **Get Started!** Write or send an e-mail message to a friend that you haven't seen in awhile. Share a verse or a lesson that you learned from your Quiet Time this week.

 Days Completed

comment corner

WE'RE PROUD OF YOU • stay with it • KEEP TRYING • BE FAITHFUL • you can do it • YOU ARE SPECIAL • keep going • KEEP IT UP • GOD LOVES YOU!

Parent or Leader, circle a comment and/or write your own.

Week 10

The Shepherd Boy Who Became King

Does your name have a meaning? David and Bathsheba named their son Solomon which means *peace*. The prophet Nathan called Solomon, Jedidiah, which means *loved by the Lord*.

SUNDAY
2 Samuel 5:1-10

David is king!
God uses ordinary people to do great things for Him. Color the crown and add jewels to it.

Write the name of the city where David ruled.

_____ (v. 7)

If you are a Christian, you are a child of the "King of kings." The greatest thing that you can do is share the gospel with someone this week.

MONDAY
2 Samuel 9:1-13

King David took in Jonathan's son, Mephibosheth, as a member of his own family. List 3 ways you can help others who have special needs.

1. _____
2. _____
3. _____

Ask a parent if you can do an act of kindness for a person who has a disability.

TUESDAY
2 Samuel 11:1-13

Color in the dotted areas to find out what King David did.

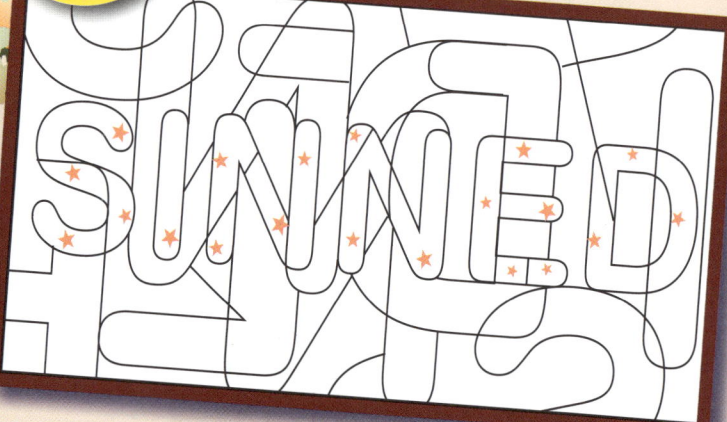

David sinned by looking at something he shouldn't have and taking something that didn't belong to him.

Computers and televisions can have good or bad pictures on them. Are you making good choices about what you allow yourself to look at? Write down what you will do when something bad comes up on the screen.

_____

WEDNESDAY
2 Samuel 11:14-18;27-28

Fill in the blanks.
One sin often leads to another – that was true in King David's case. King David planned someone else's murder.

Who did he have placed on the front lines to be killed? _____ (v. 15)
Was the man killed? _____ (v. 17)
Who sent King David a full account of the battle? _____ (v. 18)
Uriah's wife became whose wife? _____ (v. 27)

 Sin always has consequences. Write down a consequence you had from the last time you sinned (felt ashamed, guilty, got punished,...) _____ _____ Ask God for forgiveness.

THURSDAY
2 Samuel 12:1-14

Complete the crossword puzzle using the clues provided.

ACROSS
1. Man killed (v. 9)
4. Sent to David (v. 1)

DOWN
2. Type of man (v. 2)
3. The Lord took this away (v. 14)
5. David's emotion (v. 5)

 Have you said or done something bad this week? God heard it or saw it. Ask God to forgive you now.

FRIDAY
2 Samuel 12:15-23

True or False
____ 1. David fasted and prayed for his son while he was ill.
____ 2. The child lived after being sick for seven days.
____ 3. The servants were afraid to tell David that the child had died.
____ 4. After the child died, David would not eat.

Solomon

God gave David another son named Solomon. What do you know about Solomon when he grew up and became king?
_____
_____

SATURDAY
2 Samuel 23:2-4

One who rules over men must be just and right and rule in the fear of God. Draw a picture of the scene David describes in verse 4.

 Your leaders need your prayers to rule justly. Put the name of your country's leader on your Saturday prayer page, and pray that he will make wise choices.

---

comment corner

WE'RE PROUD OF YOU • stay with it • KEEP TRYING BE FAITHFUL • you can do it • YOU ARE SPECIAL • keep going • KEEP IT UP • GOD LOVES YOU!

Parent or Leader, circle a comment and/or write your own.

Days Completed

Week 11

Faith – Dead or Alive?

How would you like to have a famous brother? James was Jesus' little brother. However, James was not one of Jesus' followers until after Jesus was resurrected.

SUNDAY
James 1:2-8

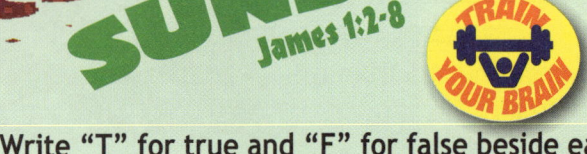

Write "T" for true and "F" for false beside each statement.

____ 1. Get angry when you face trials and temptations (v. 2).
____ 2. If you lack wisdom, ask your teacher for it (v. 5).
____ 3. The testing of faith produces patience or endurance (perseverance) (v. 3).
____ 4. A double-minded man is unstable in his ways (v. 8).

 Finish this sentence. Even though it is hard for me to

_____, I will have faith that God will help me.

MONDAY
James 1:12-17

Trace the dots to find the reward. If a person endures trials and temptations, they will receive what? (v. 12)

 Every good gift comes from whom?

_____ (v.17)

TUESDAY
James 1:22-25

Circle the correct picture. What is a *hearer* of the Word compared to?

 Are you a doer?
Did you: Yes   No
1. Do your Quiet Time every day this week?   ___   ___
2. Pray every day this week?   ___   ___
3. Memorize a verse?   ___   ___

WEDNESDAY
James 2:1-4

Circle the people you would invite to your church.

It is wrong to "play favorites" — only accepting certain children and not all. The Lord wants all children to come to know Him as Savior. Be a friend to someone you haven't accepted before.

THURSDAY
James 2:14-18

Solve the code.
Go down the letter column and across the number row to find the correct letter. For example: B1=F, C3=O.

	A	B	C
1	S	F	I
2	A	H	T
3	W	D	O

FAITH WITHOUT WORKS

_ _ _ _ _
B1 A2 C1 C2 B2

_ _ _ _ U _
A3 C1 C2 B2 C3 C2

_ _ R K _
A3 C3   A1

_ _ _ E _ _
C1 A1   B3 A2 B3

Circle Yes or No.
Yesterday I acted like a Christian.   Yes   No
Yesterday I talked like a Christian.   Yes   No

FRIDAY
James 2:19-26

Five words to never forget.
Write the similar five words that are repeated by James in verses 20 and 26.

_____
_____
_____
_____

Who else believes in God? (v.19)
_____

What was Abraham called in verse 23?
_____

Show others your faith by the works you do. Draw a heart by each day in your Quiet Time this week in which you served others.

SATURDAY
James 3:2-6

Talk about the Tongue
Draw a picture that shows how the tongue is described in these verses.

Verse 3   Verse 4   Verse 6

Your words can either help or hurt others. Think about how you treated your family this week.
Were the words you used:
   HELPFUL   or   HURTFUL ?
         Circle one.

---

comment corner

  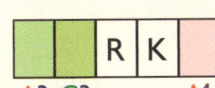 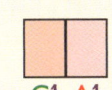 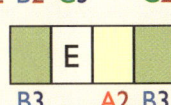

WE'RE PROUD OF YOU | stay with it | KEEP TRYING BE FAITHFUL | you can do it | YOU ARE SPECIAL | keep going | KEEP IT UP | GOD LOVES YOU!

Days Completed

Parent or Leader, circle a comment and/or write your own.

Week 12

The Godly Way or the Worldly Way?

How many pieces of clothing are you wearing? The average Jewish man wore five items of clothing: an outer garment (cloak), an inner garment (long shirt), a belt, headwear, and sandals.

SUNDAY
James 3:13-18

Find the words that describe both kinds of wisdom.

- DEVILISH
- PURE
- GENTLE
- GOOD FRUITS
- EARTHLY
- PEACEABLE
- FULL OF MERCY

```
F P D C E P C K F C
U H B E U U Z Z J H
L T Z O V R J E N S
L D Z J A I L I T E
O P L J X T L F A A
F N O K N W U I Q R
M F L E S R J P S T
E A G G F P U R E H
R S M D Q U A C M L
C J O B S O S P R Y
Y O B I U E W N R L
G P E A C E A B L E
```

Wisdom comes from listening to God's Word. This week, take notes when your pastor preaches.

MONDAY
James 4:1-4

Circle the one with whom you choose to be a friend.

WORLD   GOD

Circle the things that you love as much or more than God. Cross out the rest.

Friends   **Fun**   **Money**
Toys   **Computer**   **TV**

TUESDAY
James 4:6-10

Fill in the missing letters.

Su⬤mi⬤ to ⬤od.
R⬤sist the ⬤evil,
and he ⬤ill ⬤lee
f⬤om ⬤ou.

Do you know what *resist* means? It means to stand up to or hold up against something or someone. Write one way that you will resist the devil when you are tempted today or this week.

_____

WEDNESDAY
James 4:13-17

How Long Will You Live?
1. Verse 14 compares life to a _____
2. What happens to a vapor or mist? _____
3. Verse 17 says that if we know to do good and don't do it, we _____.

Write Yes or No.
Did you choose to disobey your parents or teachers this week? _____
Did you try to make excuses for yourself? _____
If you did, confess it and make it right with them.

THURSDAY
James 5:1-3

What Happens to a Rich Man's Stuff?
Draw lines to match the material things with the words that describe them.

Riches or wealth — moth-eaten
Garments or clothes — rusted, corroded, or cankered
Gold and silver — corrupted or rotted

 Instead of spending your allowance or birthday money on yourself, give an offering to a missionary with a need. Ask your parent or leader for suggestions.

FRIDAY
James 5:10-12

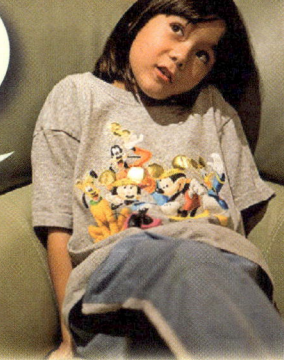

Reread the last half of verse 12. This verse says that you are to let your _____ be _____ and your _____ be _____.

"Always tell the truth."

Have you ever told a lie? _____
Make a promise to your parents that you will try to tell the truth all week. Ask them to check back with you next week to see if you kept your promise.

SATURDAY
James 5:13-16

 Write down the number of times you see the word **PRAY** or **PRAYER** in these verses. _____
Write down at least four times during your day when you can pray.
_____ _____
_____ _____

 Write down how many minutes you prayed today.
_____

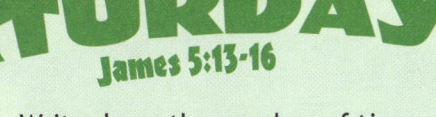

comment corner — WE'RE PROUD OF YOU — stay with it — KEEP TRYING BE FAITHFUL — you can do it — YOU ARE SPECIAL — keep going — KEEP IT UP — GOD LOVES YOU!

Days Completed

Parent or Leader, circle a comment and/or write your own.

Week 13

Got Wisdom?

In order to help the poor, the Jews put food like bread, beans, and fruit in a poor bowl daily. A poor basket was used for collecting clothes and food weekly.

SUNDAY
Proverbs 21:2-8

There is only one solution for the Christian. Follow the red letters to find the answer. Write the letters in order in the spaces to find out how God wants you to act each day.

_ _ _ _ _ _ _ _ _

You obey God by obeying those in charge over you. Write one way you will obey today.

_____

MONDAY
Proverbs 21:20-22

Being wise is more than knowing many facts. It is using what you have in the best way you can. Circle the phrases describing the best way to use what is in the picture.

- spend it foolishly.
- save it wisely.
- give it to meet someone's needs.

- closed on the shelf
- opened and read every day

- helping others
- hitting someone

Good job choosing to read your Bible today! Finish this sentence. I will help _____ by _____ _____.

TUESDAY
Proverbs 21:23-26

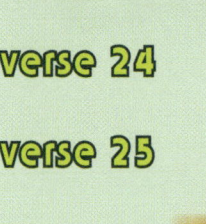

Draw a line to match the verse to the picture it describes.

verse 23

verse 24

verse 25

verse 26

Are there some attitudes or actions that need to change in your life? Pray and ask God to help you right now.

WEDNESDAY
Proverbs 22:1-9

Answer the following questions.

1. What is better than great riches (wealth)? _____
2. The Lord is the maker of what two groups of people? _____ _____
3. What three rewards will you get from humility and fearing the Lord? _____ _____ _____
4. Who needs training? _____
5. The _____ is the servant (slave) to the _____.

GET STARTED! Write down one thing you have learned from Proverbs that will help you now and when you are older.
_____

THURSDAY
Proverbs 22:17-18

Be WISE not a WISE GUY!
Fill in the missing letters to see how you can get and use wise words.

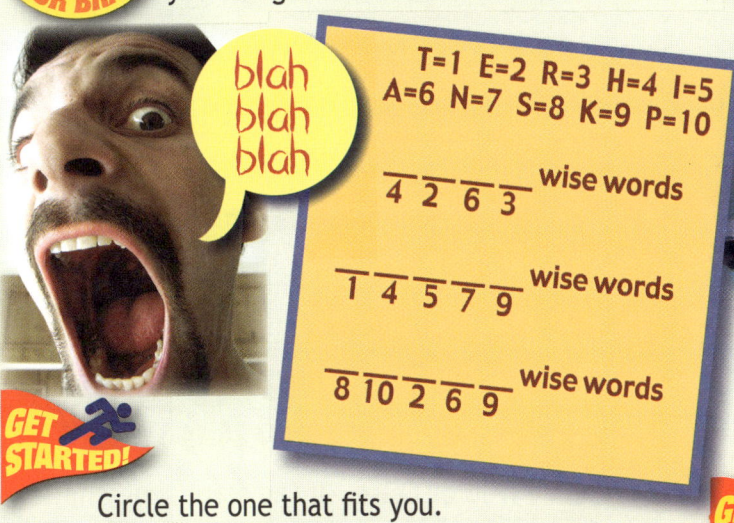

T=1 E=2 R=3 H=4 I=5
A=6 N=7 S=8 K=9 P=10

__ __ __ __ wise words
 4 2 6 3

__ __ __ __ __ wise words
 1 4 5 7 9

__ __ __ __ __ wise words
 8 10 2 6 9

Circle the one that fits you.
I use wise words most of the time.
I need to be more careful with my words.

FRIDAY
Proverbs 23:12

Draw a line from the ear to the best ways for you to hear words of knowledge.

GET STARTED! Where are you hearing most of your knowledge from? _____

SATURDAY
Proverbs 23:22-25

GET STARTED!
On a scale of 1-5
with 1 being not wise at all
to 5 being very wise,
how would you grade yourself? 1 2 3 4 5
How would your parents grade you? 1 2 3 4 5

What will your father and mother do when they see that you have wisdom? Fill in the marked sections to see the word.

---

comment corner WE'RE PROUD OF YOU stay with it KEEP TRYING BE FAITHFUL you can do it YOU ARE SPECIAL keep going KEEP IT UP GOD LOVES YOU!

Days Completed

Parent or Leader, circle a comment and/or write your own.

Week 14 — God Rejoices When You Make Right Choices

Lions and bears, oh my! They were a serious problem in Israel. Lions and bears not only attacked livestock but people as well.

SUNDAY
Proverbs 23:29-35

Write down from each of the verses what happens to a person who loves to drink alcohol.

Verse 29 **What does the person look like?**
_____

Verse 32 **What does it feel like?**
_____

Verse 33 **What does the person see?**
_____

Verse 35 **What will the person do when he wakes up?**
_____

GET STARTED! Does this sound like a way you would like to live? YES NO
Ask God right now to help you make choices that will keep your body healthy.

MONDAY
Proverbs 24:1-2, 5-8

Who would you choose as your friends? Follow the lines from the letters to discover the two groups of people. Then circle the group you want as your friends.

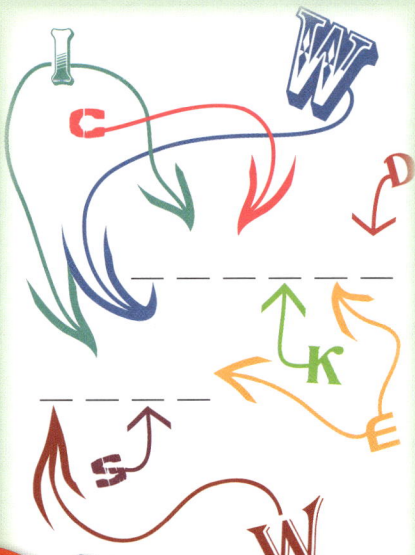

GET STARTED!
Who is your best friend? _____
Is that person a Christian who lives wisely?   YES NO

TUESDAY
Proverbs 24:19-22

True or False. If the statement is false, change the incorrect word(s) and write the correct word on the line.

_____ 1. Don't envy the wicked. _____

_____ 2. The lamp or the candle of the wicked will be bright. _____

_____ 3. Fear the wicked person. _____

_____ 4. Wicked people will have sudden calamity or destruction. _____

 **GET STARTED!** Trouble loves company. Make a choice today to stay away from people who make trouble.

WEDNESDAY
Proverbs 24:30-34

A farmer planted a field but did not take care of it. The vineyard became broken down. Find the hidden letters in the picture of the word which describes a sluggard or slothful person.

Circle the areas in which you could work a little harder.

Doing my homework.   Cleaning my room.   Doing my chores.   Doing my Quiet Time.   Obeying right away with the right spirit.

THURSDAY
Proverbs 25:2-7

A king makes many important decisions each day. In order for the king to go through the maze wisely to the castle, he must get his Bible and the book of laws.

Put the names of your country's leaders on today's prayer page. Pray for them faithfully

FRIDAY
Proverbs 25:11-14

Match the pictures to what it describes.

- A faithful messenger that the master is refreshed to see.
- A wise reproof or rebuke to someone who is listening.
- A person boasts about giving a false gift.
- A word spoken at the right time.

How would you describe your listening skills in church? Circle the one which fits you.

I don't listen.   I listen sometimes.   I listen and take notes of the message.

SATURDAY
Proverbs 25:21-22

How should you treat your enemies? Circle the picture that answers the questions.

1. When your enemy is hungry, what should you give him?

2. When your enemy is thirsty, what should you give him?

Does someone come to mind that treats you like an enemy? What could you do to show God's love to this person? I could

_____

comment corner

WE'RE PROUD OF YOU   stay with it   KEEP TRYING   BE FAITHFUL   you can do it   YOU ARE SPECIAL   keep going   KEEP IT UP   GOD LOVES YOU!

Parent or Leader, circle a comment and/or write your own.

Days Completed

Week 15

Submit to the Savior

Jesus called Peter, Cephas which means rock. Jesus gave him this name to describe how strong Peter would need to be for his future ministry.

SUNDAY
1 Peter 1:3-5

God has an inheritance (treasure) in Heaven waiting for each of His children (v. 4). If you have accepted Christ as your Savior, you will receive your inheritance someday. Write your name on the treasure chest and color it.

GET STARTED! Ask your parents to explain what an inheritance is. Circle the inheritance that will last forever.

heavenly inheritance   earthly inheritance

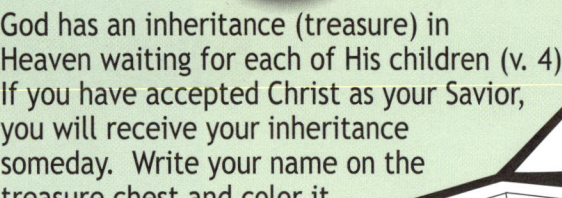

MONDAY
1 Peter 1:13-16

Color in the dotted spaces to find the word that tells you how God wants you to behave.

TUESDAY
1 Peter 1:18-21, 25

Cross out the picture that does not answer either question.
What redeems you (v. 19)?
What lasts forever (v. 25)?

GET STARTED! Finish the sentence. One way I can live a holy life for God is by _____.

GET STARTED! Share your favorite verse with a friend.

WEDNESDAY
1 Peter 2:1-6

When you accept Christ as your Savior, you are like what? _____

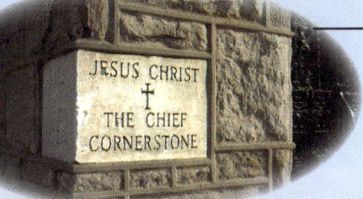

According to verse 6, Jesus is the _____ of the building of God's family.

 Put a check before each sentence that is true for you.

____ I did my Quiet Time yesterday.
____ I did my Quiet Time today.
____ I plan to do my Quiet Time tomorrow.

THURSDAY
1 Peter 2:13-17

Your government leaders make laws for you to follow. Below are signs you are to obey. Draw a line from the sign to its meaning.

- Seatbelts Required
- School Crossing
- No Smoking
- Fire Exit
- Poison

 Do you pray for the leaders in your government? Write the name of the leader of your country on your Thursday prayer page and faithfully pray for him.

FRIDAY
1 Peter 2:18-23

 Even though these verses are talking about slaves, you can apply them to those who are in authority over you. Answer Yes or No to the following questions.

____ 1. Only listen to people in charge over you if they are good to you (v. 18).

____ 2. God is pleased when you suffer patiently even if you were right, and the people over you were wrong (vv. 19-20).

____ 3. When people were unkind to Jesus, He did not fight back with His words or actions (vv. 22-23).

 Write the grade that each person would give you for the way you show respect to them.
____ Parents   ____ Teachers
____ Sunday school teacher

SATURDAY
1 Peter 3:1-7

How should husbands and wives treat each other?

Verse 1 – **Wives are to be** _____.

Verse 7 – **Husbands are to** _____.

Verses 3-4 – **Is it important to be beautiful on the inside (hidden) or outside?** _____

 Even though you are young, you can begin praying now for your future husband or wife. Take a few minutes right now to ask God to help you make good choices about your friends.

comment corner — WE'RE PROUD OF YOU · stay with it · KEEP TRYING BE FAITHFUL · you can do it · YOU ARE SPECIAL · keep going · KEEP IT UP · GOD LOVES YOU!

Parent or Leader, circle a comment and/or write your own.

Days Completed

Week 16 — Strength in Suffering

Peter's ministry lasted about thirty years. He was martyred in A.D. 67.

SUNDAY
1 Peter 3:8-12

Draw a line from the verse to all the body parts that it describes.

Verse 10

Verse 12

 On a scale of 1-5 (1 being very bad and 5 being excellent), write down the number that describes your:
____ attitude   ____ words   ____ actions

MONDAY
1 Peter 3:13-17

We are told in verse 15 to be ready to give a(n) _____.
To find the answer, color the letters that spell the word.

 Have you ever been punished even though you did nothing wrong? How did you feel? Jesus suffered on the cross for you even though He never did anything wrong.

TUESDAY
1 Peter 4:1-2

Since Christ already suffered for you, how should you live? Find the path in the maze that leads you to the right answer.

FLESH

EVIL HUMAN DESIRES

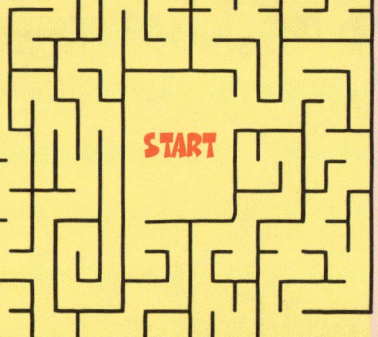

WILL OF GOD

 Jesus suffered a cruel death for you. How often do you thank Jesus for dying on the cross for your sins? Circle one.

All the time   Once in a while   Never

WEDNESDAY
1 Peter 4:8-11

TRAIN YOUR BRAIN — Answer the following questions.

1. What covers a multitude of sins? (v. 8) _____
2. You should show hospitality to others without (v. 9) _____
3. Who are you to serve with the gift God gives you? (v. 10) _____

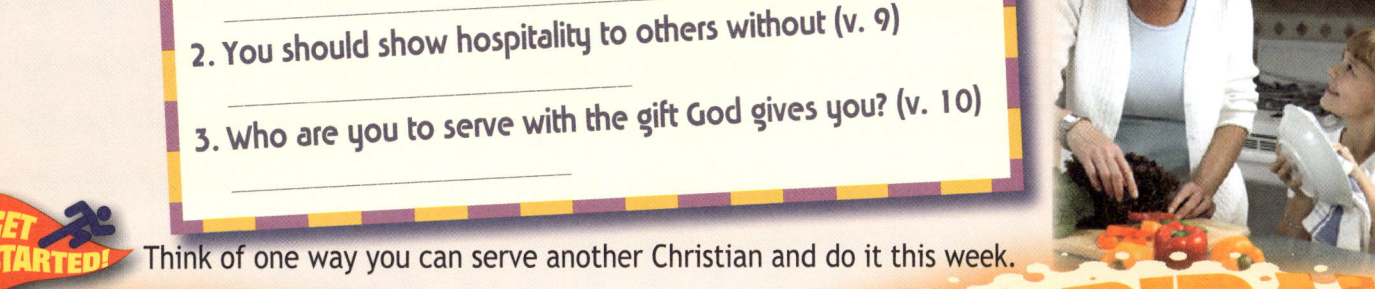

GET STARTED! Think of one way you can serve another Christian and do it this week.

THURSDAY
1 Peter 4:12-16

TRAIN YOUR BRAIN — Fill in the blanks. Use the verses to finish the statements.

If we suffer for Christ, we can r _ _ _ _ _ _ e (v. 13).

If you suffer as a Christian, don't be _ _ s _ _ _ _ d (v. 16).

GET STARTED! Share with a parent or leader about a hard time in your life and how God helped you.

FRIDAY
1 Peter 5:1-3, 7

TRAIN YOUR BRAIN — An elder is a _____ of a church.

Verse 2 talks about taking care of the flock of God. Who takes care of a flock of sheep?

Read Isaiah 53:6 — We are like _____.

GET STARTED! Your pastor has a big job of studying God's Word to teach your church family. Write him a thank-you note this week to tell him how much you appreciate all he does.

SATURDAY
1 Peter 5:8-10

TRAIN YOUR BRAIN — Who is compared to a roaring lion? Write the answer in the blank provided. Color the lion.

_____

GET STARTED! Verse 9 says you can defeat the lion by being steadfast or firm in your faith. Finish this sentence: I can stand firm in my faith and resist temptation by _____.

Comment Corner

WE'RE PROUD OF YOU • stay with it • KEEP TRYING BE FAITHFUL • you can do it • YOU ARE SPECIAL • keep going • KEEP IT UP • GOD LOVES YOU!

Days Completed

Parent or Leader, circle a comment and/or write your own.

Week 17 — Told By an Angel

Although Joseph was just a simple carpenter, he was related to royalty. He was a member of the tribe of Judah and could trace his family line to King David.

SUNDAY
Luke 1:1-12

Train Your Brain

Luke was an investigator. He only told the true facts about Jesus. Pretend you are a detective. What questions would you want to ask Luke about Jesus?

_____
_____
_____

Get Started!

Talk to an adult and ask him to share something from his life when he was a young Christian.

MONDAY
Luke 1:13-20

Train Your Brain

Do the crossword puzzle.

ACROSS
4 Wife of Zacharias
5 What Zacharias could not do until John was born.

DOWN
1 Person to whom the angel appeared
2 A drink John could not have
3 The name they were to call their baby

Get Started!

An angel will never come to tell you what to do. List three people God wants you to listen to and obey.

_____
_____
_____

TUESDAY
Luke 1:26-35

Train Your Brain

Rearrange the word tiles to find the message from today's verses.

WILL · NAME · SON · JESUS · BIRTH · HIM · MARY

_____ _____ give _____ to God's _____ and _____ _____ _____.

Get Started!

God can do the impossible if He chooses. Pray for the people on your Tuesday prayer page. If you do not have any, write some in the spaces.

WEDNESDAY
Luke 1:46-56

Mary praises God in verses 46-56. Fill in each star with an important word from the verses. The first letter is given to you.

- R _ _ _ _ _ _ _ v. 47
- B _ _ _ _ _ _ _ v. 48
- M _ _ _ _ v. 49
- M _ _ _ _ v. 50
- F _ _ _ _ _ v. 53
- I _ _ _ _ _ v. 54

Fill in your praises on the prayer pages of your Quiet Time. Share your praises with a friend or family member.

THURSDAY
Luke 1:57-66

Answer the questions below.

1. Why did Zacharias and Elizabeth name their son John? (Luke 1:13.)
   _____

2. Why was Zacharias able to speak again in verse 64? (Luke 1:18-20.)
   _____
   _____

Talk with your parents about how your name was chosen for you. Does your name have a special meaning? Write it here.
_____

FRIDAY
Luke 1:76-80

Zacharias said his son John would have a very important job to do (vv. 76-77). Unscramble the letters to find the words.

John would (reppare) _ _ _ _ _ _ _ the way for the Lord and give the people the (egdelwonk) _ _ _ _ _ _ _ _ _ of salvation.

You can help someone to hear about Jesus, too. Write the name of a friend you will invite to church this week.
_____

SATURDAY
Luke 2:1-7

Find the names and places in the word search.

This wasn't any easy trip. Why did Mary and Joseph have to go to Bethlehem?
_____

Do you have the right attitude when you are asked to do something which is hard for you? Circle the word that fits for you.

Often **Sometimes** **Never**

Roman, Joseph, Mary, Caesar, Bethlehem, David, Judea, Nazareth

```
F X R G N B U M Y J
B U E L N E A A Q O
Q J R A O T K R L S
B J M C R H A Y G E
D O A B A L Z J G P
R A J U D E A B B H
Y B V H U H S R E Y
X L A I M E I A L O
O H A O D M J T R G
N A Z A R E T H V Z
```

comment corner
WE'RE PROUD OF YOU · stay with it · KEEP TRYING · BE FAITHFUL · you can do it · YOU ARE SPECIAL · keep going · KEEP IT UP · GOD LOVES YOU!

Parent or Leader, circle a comment and/or write your own.

Days Completed

Week 18

The Family Tree of Jesus

How would you like riding on a donkey over bumpy rocky roads for 90 miles? That's how far it was from Nazareth to Bethlehem.

SUNDAY
Luke 2:15-20

Color in the starred sections to find out one of the first groups to see Mary, Joseph, and baby Jesus. Where did they go and what did they do after they saw Jesus? They went to _____ to _____.

SHEPHERDS

GET STARTED! Write down the names of people and places where you have shared the Gospel. _____ _____ _____

MONDAY
Luke 2:25-30, 36-38

God allowed two people to see their Redeemer Jesus before they died. Write their names under their pictures.

TUESDAY
Luke 2:41-52

Number the events in order.

___ Joseph, Mary, and Jesus returned to Nazareth.
___ Joseph, Mary, and Jesus went to Jerusalem for the feast of the Passover.
___ Joseph and Mary found Jesus teaching in the temple.
___ Jesus stayed in Jerusalem.
___ Joseph and Mary thought Jesus was with relatives and headed for home.

___ ___ ___ ___ ___ ___ ___

___ ___ ___ ___ ___ ___ ___

GET STARTED! Write the names of two older adults in your church who are faithful Christians.

_____
_____

Write a note of thanks to them for their faithfulness and for being a good example to you.

GET STARTED! Was Jesus disobedient to Mary and Joseph? **YES NO**
Your parents would worry if you were lost. Discuss a plan with them on what to do if you get lost.

50

Week 19 — The Son of Man Seeks

A *hazzan* was responsible for the safe keeping of the scrolls of Scripture read in the synagogue. In Luke 4:20, Jesus handed the Isaiah scroll to a *hazzan* after He finished reading it.

SUNDAY
Luke 4:16-24

TRAIN YOUR BRAIN — Circle the correct answers.

Where was Jesus? Bethlehem **Nazareth** Jerusalem

Jesus read from what book of the Bible? Jeremiah Luke Isaiah

Jesus came to preach to which three groups of people?

How was Jesus received in Nazareth? Accepted Rejected

GET STARTED! Jesus was not welcome in His hometown. Have you ever been teased or picked on for being a Christian? YES NO Talk to a parent or older Christian friend about what to do.

MONDAY
Luke 4:31-40

TRAIN YOUR BRAIN — Color the frames the same to match the persons on the left with what Jesus did for them on the right.

A man in the synagogue in Capernaum	Called unclean spirit to come out of him
Simon's mother-in-law	Laid hands on them and healed them
Sick brought to Jesus at Simon's home	Healed her fever

GET STARTED! Have you ever prayed that Jesus would heal someone? YES NO How did Jesus answer your prayers? _____ Talk to a parent or leader about this time.

TUESDAY
Luke 5:4-11

TRAIN YOUR BRAIN — Jesus caught fish to show the disciples they would now be catching men for Christ. Write a name of a Christian in each fish to represent people *caught* for Christ.

GET STARTED! Whom are you praying for to be *caught for Christ*? _____

WEDNESDAY
Luke 5:12-20

 Jesus healed two people. Draw a line from the statement to the person it describes.

LEPER   Jesus forgave this man's sins.
PARALYZED (PALSY) MAN   Jesus touched this man to heal him.

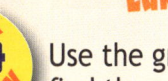 What is more important? Circle one.
Healthy saved heart
Healthy sinful heart

THURSDAY
Luke 5:27-32

 Use the grid puzzle to find the missing letters.

	1	2	3
★	S	R	E
◆	G	N	H
✳	T	O	U

Jesus said that He did not call the
_ _ _ _ _ _ _ _
★2 ◆1 ◆3 ✳1 ★3 ✳2 ✳3 ★1
but
_ _ _ _ _ _ _
★1 ◆2 ◆2 ★3 ★2 ★1
to repentance.

 Do you think that you are better than others because you are a Christian? **Yes No** Remember to be kind to all people you meet.

FRIDAY
Luke 6:1-5

 Write the letters in between the X's in the boxes below to reveal the hidden message.

TXXXHEXXXSXAXBXBXAXTXHXXXWAXXXSX
AXXXJXEXWXIXSXXXXHXXXXDAXXXYXXOFX
RXEXSXTXAXNXXXDXXWXOXRSXXXHXIXXPXX

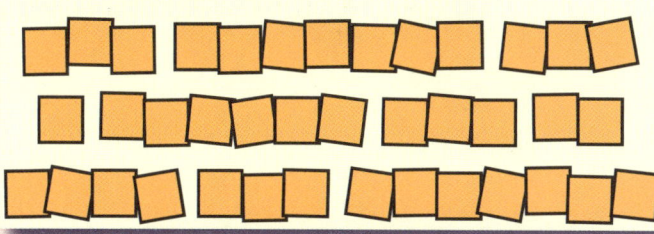

Christians set Sunday aside as a special day for Jesus. What do you do on Sunday to worship or glorify God? _____

SATURDAY
Luke 6:13-16

 Find the names of the twelve apostles in verses 14-16 and write them on the lines. (Hint: Some apostles have the same names.)

S____ P____ A____ J____ J____ P____ B____

M____ T____ J____ S____ J____ J____ I____

After you have written their names, see if you can say them without looking.

comment corner — WE'RE PROUD OF YOU · stay with it · KEEP TRYING · BE FAITHFUL · you can do it · YOU ARE SPECIAL · keep going · KEEP IT UP · GOD LOVES YOU!

Days Completed

Parent or Leader, circle a comment and/or write your own.

Week 20

In the Dark? Follow the Son!

Jewish homes used their flat roofs for many purposes like praying, cooking, and making announcements. For safety reasons, fences around the roof were required by Mosaic Law (Deut. 22:8).

SUNDAY
Luke 6:27-36

Color in the marked sections to see whom you need to love.

Verse 31 is often called the Golden Rule. Write it in your own words.

_____
_____

MONDAY
Luke 6:39-45

Circle the correct answer. Write the verse number which answers the question.

Yes No Can a blind man lead another blind man? Verse _____

Yes No Are we to judge others? Verses _____

Yes No Can a corrupt/bad tree have good fruit? Verse _____

Yes No Does a good man treasure evil? Verse _____

Are you building your life on Jesus Christ? Tell a Christian adult about when you asked Christ into your heart. If you have never asked Christ into your heart, talk to a Christian adult about how you can do that.

TUESDAY
Luke 7:1-10

Place the missing vowels to finish the statement.

TH_ S_RV_NT
W_ S H_ _L D
B_ C_ _S_ _F TH_
C_NT_R__N'S
GR__T F__TH.

A E I O U

This man had great faith. Circle the word that comes closest to describing your faith.

**NO FAITH   WEAK FAITH
STRONG FAITH**

54

WEDNESDAY
Luke 7:18-23

Fill in the blanks to show how Jesus healed the people in the list. Reread verse 22 if you do not remember.

The blind _____
The lame _____
Lepers _____
The deaf _____
The dead _____
The poor _____

GET STARTED! Jesus can still heal people today. Do you know anyone Jesus has healed from a sickness? Yes   No   Pray now, thanking Jesus for His healing power.

THURSDAY
Luke 7:24-30

Cross out all the Q's. Write the hidden message on the lines.

_____
_____
_____.

JQQOHQNQQPQRQEQPQARQQQQEDQ
QQQQTHQQEQQWQAQQYFQQOQRQ
QQJQQQQEQSQUQQQS.

GET STARTED! Would others call you God's messenger?   Yes   No

FRIDAY
Luke 7:36-50

Draw a line from the person to the action that describes him or her.

- Washed feet of Jesus with her hair and tears
- Told parable of money lender
- Gave no water to Jesus to wash His feet
- Forgave woman's sins
- Gave no kiss to Jesus
- Anointed feet of Jesus with perfume
- Answered Jesus about parable

GET STARTED! Name a gift you have given to Jesus.
_____

SATURDAY
Luke 8:5-15

Write the letter from the list in column B next to the item in Column A to explain the meaning of Jesus' parable. Reread verses 11-15 if you need help.

Column A
___ Seed
___ Beside the road or path/ on the wayside
___ On rocks or rocky soil
___ Among thorns
___ Good soil or ground

Column B
A. Hear and believe the Word but fall away from God
B. Word of God/ Bible
C. Hear the Word of God but choked out by life's worries or cares
D. Hear the Word of God and keep it
E. Hear the Word, but do not believe

GET STARTED! Which soil are you? _____

comment corner: WE'RE PROUD OF YOU · stay with it · KEEP TRYING · BE FAITHFUL · you can do it · YOU ARE SPECIAL · keep going · KEEP IT UP · GOD LOVES YOU!

Parent or Leader, circle a comment and/or write your own.

Days Completed

55

Week 21: Jesus' Power Proves His Position

At 200 feet deep, the Sea of Galilee is considered rather shallow which is why the winds can easily whip up the waves and cause dangerous storms. The Sea of Galilee is also 68 stories lower than any ocean.

SUNDAY
Luke 8:22-25

Find the words in the word search.

- ASLEEP
- FAITH
- LAKE
- OBEY
- SHIP
- STORM
- WATER
- WINDS

```
A S D N I W L
D S S F H A O
F J L T K T B
K Y I E O E E
B A P M E R Y
F V S H I P M
C Q L Z X N S
```

Use the colored letters to spell out the name that the disciples called Jesus.
_ _ _ _ _ _   Do you use that name for God?   YES   NO

MONDAY
Luke 8:26-40

Draw a line from the statement to the word BEFORE or AFTER Jesus healed the man.

- The people of Gadarenes (Gerasenes) wanted Jesus to leave.
- The demons (devils) went into the swine.
- He said his name was Legion.
- He was living in the tombs.
- Jesus told the man to return to his house.
- The man was in his right mind.

BEFORE

AFTER

If you have accepted Jesus as your Savior, write a word that describes you *before* you knew Him.
_____
Write a word that describes you *after*.
_____
If you can't do this, talk to your parents or pastor.

TUESDAY
Luke 8:41-56

Answer each question to reveal what we need to have in Christ.

1. Jarius fell at the ___ of Jesus.
2. What does Peter call Jesus in verse 45?
3. What was returned to the child in verse 55?
4. Who answers Jesus in verse 45?
5. Who entered with Jesus, Peter and James in Verse 51?

These people showed great faith in Jesus. Who else have you read about in the Bible that showed great faith?
_____

WEDNESDAY
Luke 9:1-11

Use the code to complete the message.

You can share the message of Jesus, too. Who can you invite to church next week? Begin praying for them today.

THURSDAY
Luke 9:12-17

Answer each question with a number from today's verses.

How many loaves of bread were there? _____
How many fish did they have? _____
How many men did Jesus feed? _____
How many baskets of food were left over? _____

You can help feed the hungry in your town. Talk to your parents and neighbors about donating food to the local food pantry.

FRIDAY
Luke 9:28-36

God the Father speaks from a cloud in verse 35. Write the message He gives in the cloud below.

One way you can listen to God is by reading the Bible and doing your Quiet Time. What is another way you will listen to God today? _____
_____

SATURDAY
Luke 9:43-48

Circle the letters of the words that tell what the disciples didn't understand about Jesus.

The Son of Man (Jesus) will be _____ into the hands of men.

Jesus told them that whoever is _____ among them will be the _____.

D B E L T I R V A E Y R E D

G R L E A T E S T

Do you try to be first at recess, playing games, or getting snacks? Starting today, allow someone else to be first.

comment corner
WE'RE PROUD OF YOU • stay with it • KEEP TRYING BE FAITHFUL • you can do it • YOU ARE SPECIAL • keep going • KEEP IT UP • GOD LOVES YOU!

Days Completed

Parent or Leader, circle a comment and/or write your own.

Week 22 — The Seventy Sent Forth

Jews and Samaritans really didn't like each other. The Samaritans were people of mixed race, Jew and Gentile. In order for the Jews to get to Galilee, they had to pass through Samaria.

SUNDAY — Luke 9:51-56

 People have all sorts of excuses why they reject Christ as their Savior. Write a reason why someone would reject Him in each speaking bubble.

"I have my own religion."

 Look again at what Jesus says in verse 56. Should you get angry at people who give you excuses for not wanting to accept Christ as their Savior? _____

MONDAY — Luke 10:1-6

How many men did Jesus send out as missionaries? _____
How many men were supposed to be in each group going out? _____
Write the name of a missionary you know or one your church supports. _____

Get Started! Write a letter or e-mail to the missionary that you listed above. Put his or her name on your Monday prayer page.

TUESDAY — Luke 10:13-16

Fit the cities into the criss-cross.

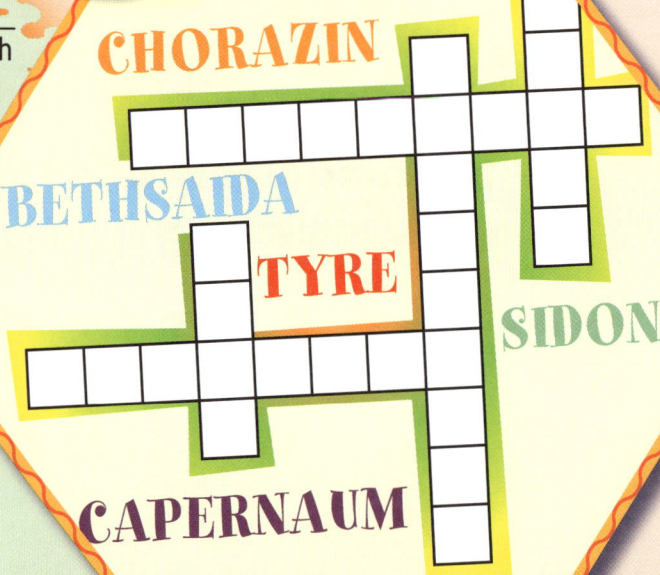

CHORAZIN BETHSAIDA TYRE SIDON CAPERNAUM

Get Started! When you talk to someone about the Gospel and he rejects it, who is he really rejecting? You or Christ?

WEDNESDAY
Luke 10:29-37

Circle the picture of the person who was the real neighbor in the parable.

beat up man   the priest   the Levite   Good Samaritan

 Is there someone in your class whom you avoid for some reason? YES NO
This week do an act of kindness for this person. Remember, he is your neighbor.

THURSDAY
Luke 10:38-42

Both Martha and Mary loved Jesus. Write their name under their picture.

_____

_____

 Whom would you be most like? Martha who is too busy, or Mary who spends time with Jesus?
_____

FRIDAY
Luke 11:9-13

God never wants you to stop asking Him for your needs. Use the words to help you fill in the blanks.

KNOCKS   FIND   GIVEN
SEEK   ASK   OPENED

_____ and it will be _____ to you;
_____ and you will _____;
and to him who _____, it will be _____ to you.

 Your parents try to give you nice things. Are you grateful? Do you say thank you to them? God does even more for you than your parents. Thank Him today for taking such good care of you.

SATURDAY
Luke 11:28

 Fill in the blanks from Jesus' words in verse 28.

_____ are _____ who _____ the word of _____ and _____ it.

 This verse says we are to obey God. Who are some people you are to obey? _____
Ask one of the people you listed how they think you are doing on obedience.

comment corner — WE'RE PROUD OF YOU • stay with it • KEEP TRYING • BE FAITHFUL • you can do it • YOU ARE SPECIAL • keep going • KEEP IT UP • GOD LOVES YOU!

Days Completed

Parent or Leader, circle a comment and/or write your own.

Week 23

How to Have and Keep a Happy Heart

Pilate ordered Roman guards to dress in robes and kill the Galileans while they worshiped. Because of his evil act, Pilate was afraid to face the Jews, which may account for his wanting to turn Jesus over to Herod. (Luke 13)

SUNDAY
Luke 11:33-36

Train Your Brain

Answer the following questions.

- Where shouldn't you put your light? _____
- Where should you put your light? _____
- What part of your body is like a lamp? _____
- If you obey the teachings of Jesus, would your body be full of *darkness* or *light*? _____

GET STARTED! Have you ever sung the chorus, *This little light of mine, I'm going to let it shine*? It is not just a fun song to sing but a Biblical way to live. Is your light shining? YES NO

MONDAY
Luke 11:42-48

Train Your Brain

WOE is not the same WHOA that you say to stop a horse. Follow the letters in bubbles to find the meaning of WOE.

"__oe is a __rnin_ fr_m Jes_s t_ch__n_e __r wa_s."
(letters: a, g, w, o, y, u)

GET STARTED! Write down one thing Jesus could write a woe about to you (talking back to adults, whining, tattling, lying, being selfish,...) Woe to you for _____. Work on changing your ways this week.

TUESDAY
Luke 12:2-10

Train Your Brain

Black out the Z's to reveal the hidden message and write it on the lines.

ZZGODZZKNZZOZWSZ
ZEZVZEZRZYZTZHZIZNZGZ
ZIZZDZOZAZZNZDZ
ZLOZZVEZZSZZMZZEZZ

____ _____
_____
__ __ __ ____
_____ ____.

GET STARTED! There are no secrets from God. If someone tells you to keep a secret that could hurt you or another person, share it with a trusted adult. Write down the names of at least two trusted adults you could tell.

1. _____
2. _____

WEDNESDAY
Luke 12:22-34

TRAIN YOUR BRAIN

Draw a line from each item to the heart if it is a treasure for God. Cross out the item if it will draw you away from God.

GET STARTED!

Reread verse 34. What is your greatest treasure? _____
Does your treasure bring you closer to God or draw you away from God? _____

THURSDAY
Luke 12:35-40

TRAIN YOUR BRAIN

Use the code to complete the message.

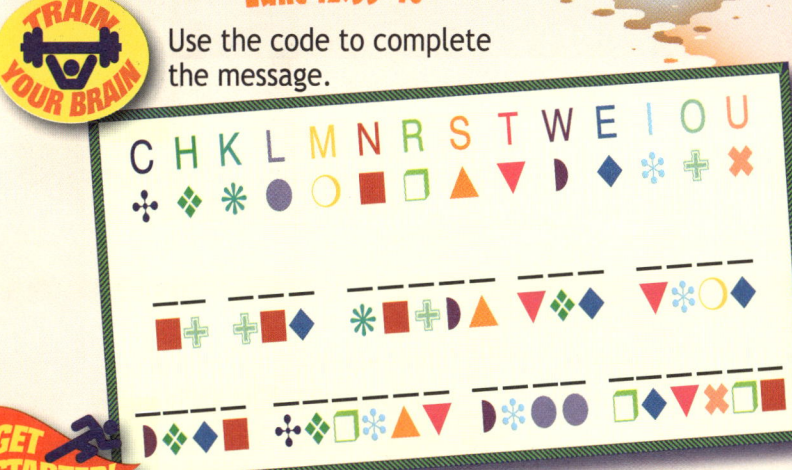

GET STARTED!

Are you ready? YES NO   Is your family ready? YES NO
Are your friends ready? YES NO
What can you do to help others be ready?
_____

FRIDAY
Luke 12:51-53

TRAIN YOUR BRAIN

Are you praying for the salvation of your unsaved family? Add their names to your prayer pages and pray for them today.

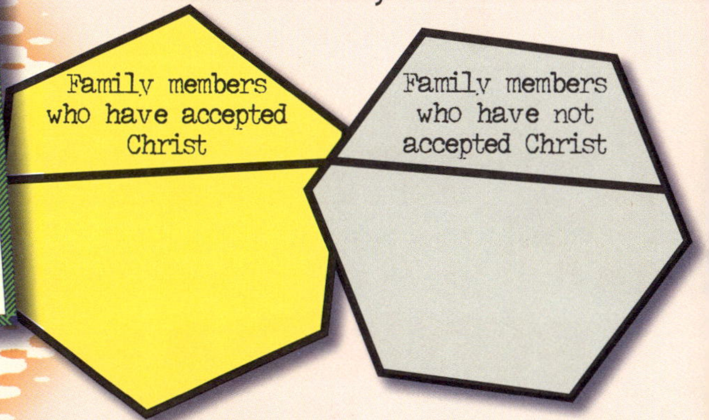

Family members who have accepted Christ

Family members who have not accepted Christ

GET STARTED!

Circle the answer that fits for you. I have **many** or **few** relatives (aunts, uncles, cousins, etc.). **Many** or **few** of my relatives are Christians. Pray for your relatives who do not know Christ as their Savior.

SATURDAY
Luke 13:1-5

TRAIN YOUR BRAIN

Both verses 3 and 5 tell you to do something. Use the clues to find the keyword from today's verses.

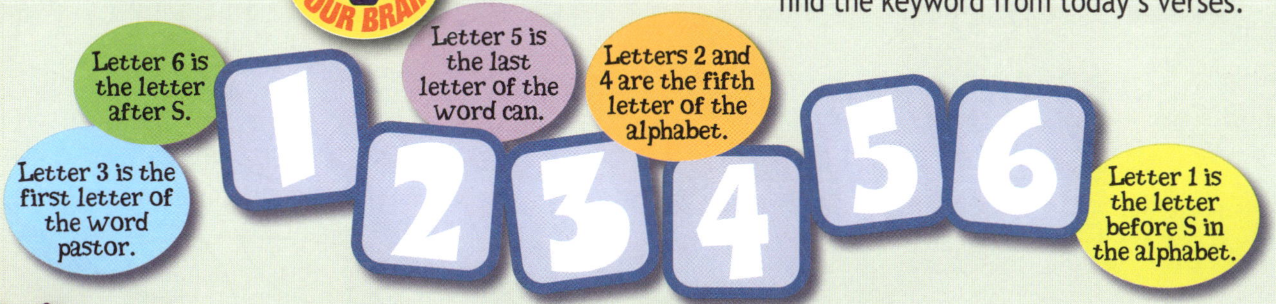

- Letter 6 is the letter after S.
- Letter 5 is the last letter of the word can.
- Letters 2 and 4 are the fifth letter of the alphabet.
- Letter 3 is the first letter of the word pastor.
- Letter 1 is the letter before S in the alphabet.

[1][2][3][4][5][6]

GET STARTED!

To repent means to admit your sin and to turn away from or stop doing the sin. Pray right now to repent from a specific sin in your life. Ask God to help you avoid the sin.

---

comment corner

WE'RE PROUD OF YOU · stay with it · KEEP TRYING · BE FAITHFUL · you can do it · YOU ARE SPECIAL · keep going · KEEP IT UP · GOD LOVES YOU!

Parent or Leader, circle a comment and/or write your own.

Days Completed

Week 24

Whose Family Comes First?

Where did the Jews get salt? They got salt from the Dead Sea which is nine times saltier than the ocean. It wasn't as good as the salt we have today, and it often turned stale.

SUNDAY — Luke 13:10-17

Train Your Brain

Circle the letter of the correct answer.

1. Where was Jesus teaching?
   - **P.** synagogue
   - **R.** in someone's house
2. How long was the woman sick?
   - **S.** 18 days
   - **R.** 18 years
3. What was wrong with the woman?
   - **B.** She was sick with the flu
   - **A.** She was bent over and couldn't get up.
4. Who was mad at Jesus for healing the woman?
   - **J.** his disciples
   - **I.** the ruler of the synagogue
5. What did Jesus call the man?
   - **S.** a hypocrite
   - **T.** a donkey
6. After Jesus answered His adversaries (opponents) they were _____.
   - **D.** delighted
   - **E.** ashamed (humiliated)

Get Started! Use the letters you circled to spell a word which shows how the ruler should have reacted to Jesus ___ ___ ___ ___ ___ ___ Check your Sunday prayer page and write in the part that says, I thank God for ....

MONDAY — Luke 13:22-27

Train Your Brain

How does one get into Heaven? Cross out the items that will not get you to Heaven, and write on the door the way to Heaven.

- eat healthy foods
- obey parents,
- give money to the poor
- exercise
- share toys
- be nice to others,
- go to a church

ONE WAY

Get Started! If you have accepted Jesus as your personal Savior, what verse is special to you?
_____
If you do not know Jesus, talk to your parents or pastor.

TUESDAY — Luke 14:7-14

Train Your Brain

Color the spaces with dots to show how Jesus wants you to act.

BE HUMBLE

Get Started! Circle the times when it is hard for you to be humble. When I ....

Win a game.

Get good grades.

Receive a compliment.

Week 25: Take What You Have Been Taught for a Walk

Call the doctor! Doctor Luke was the author of the Gospel of Luke and the book of Acts. He also was a close friend of the apostle Paul.

SUNDAY
Luke 16:13-15

Write the word *Pharisees* nearest to the thing they loved.

Write your name nearest to the thing or person you love more.

LOVER OF MONEY   LOVER OF GOD

 Money is not evil. You need it to buy food and clothes. Do not become a *lover of money*. Ask your parents for help on learning how to use money wisely.

MONDAY
Luke 16:19-31

Find the words from Heaven and Hell in the word search.

**RICH
WATER
BROTHERS
TORMENT

ABRAHAM
LAZARUS
BEGGAR**

```
X X H X X X X B
X R X C X S X R
X E X B I U X O
X T N E M R O T
X A X G X A X H
X W X G X Z X E
A B R A H A M R
X X X R X L X S
```

 Jesus told this parable (story). People on earth can't talk with people who have already died. Do not believe people or stories that say that they can.

TUESDAY
Luke 17:11-17

Write True or False.

_____ Ten lepers called out to Jesus for mercy (pity).
_____ Jesus touched the lepers and healed them.
_____ Jesus told the lepers to go show themselves to the priest.
_____ Nine lepers came back to thank Jesus.
_____ One of the lepers was a Samaritan.

 Using good manners shows that you care about others. Ask your parents to give you a grade on your manners this week. Work on practicing good manners.

WEDNESDAY
Luke 17:20-30

TRAIN YOUR BRAIN

Jesus is talking about His coming Kingdom, not the rapture. However, Christians will be going about their daily lives when the rapture happens. Fill in the clocks with the times you do these things.

 church  eat lunch  bedtime  school

 Are you ready to meet Jesus today? If not, talk to your parents or pastor.

THURSDAY
Luke 18:10-14

 **TRAIN YOUR BRAIN**

Verses 10-14 describe two very different ways to pray. Draw a line from each word or phrase to connect it to the person it describes.

- humble
- proud
- wants to be noticed by men
- wants to be heard by God

- admits to being a sinner
- brags about himself
- begs for mercy

 Which one describes you? Update your Thursday prayer pages and pray for the people on your list.

FRIDAY
Luke 18:15-17

God Loves Children!
Answer the questions below about your church.

What classes or clubs does your church have for children? (for example: Sunday school, Olympians, Vacation Bible School)
_____,
_____,
_____

Circle the ones on your list that you attend. Who are the people who help you learn about Jesus? _____

You are important to your teachers at church. Write a card or note to let them know they are important to you. Be sure to give it to them this week.

SATURDAY
Luke 18:35-43

TRAIN YOUR BRAIN Circle the correct answer.

1. What does the blind man call Jesus? (**Son of David** or **Mighty King**)
2. What does the man do when they tell him to be quiet? (**stops yelling** or **calls to Jesus again**)
3. What does the man want Jesus to do for him? (**heal him** or **talk to him**)
4. What affliction did the man want healed? (**blindness** or **deafness**)
5. What does Jesus do for the man? (**let him suffer** or **heal him**)

 God may choose to heal some people and not others. It does not mean that Jesus loves one and not the other. Whom do you know that is sick or disabled? _____. Pray for that person to honor God even in their sickness.

---

comment corner — WE'RE PROUD OF YOU · stay with it · KEEP TRYING · BE FAITHFUL · you can do it · YOU ARE SPECIAL · keep going · KEEP IT UP · GOD LOVES YOU!

Parent or Leader, circle a comment and/or write your own.

Days Completed

Week 26

The Son of Man Saves

Herod the Great built the temple in Jerusalem. It took 73 years to complete. Six years after it was done, the Romans completely destroyed it again. (Luke 21:5)

SUNDAY
Luke 19:1-10

Train Your Brain: Use the code to find the message.

A= E= I= O= U= T= S= N= R=

J◯us c◯m◯ ◯◯ s◯◯k ◯◯d ◯◯ ◯◯v◯ ◯◯n◯r◯.

J__us c_m_ __ s__k __d __ __v_ __n_r_.

Get Started! Zaccheus obeyed Jesus immediately. How is your obedience? Ask a parent or teacher how you are doing on obedience.

MONDAY
Luke 19:12-26

Train Your Brain: Circle the math symbol to show how the servants used their minas (pounds)

Servant #1 had 1 mina (pound) + - ___ minas (pounds) = ___

Servant #2 had 1 mina (pound) + - ___ minas (pounds) = ___

Servant #3 had 1 mina (pound) + - ___ minas (pounds) = ___

Circle the servants who pleased the master. Cross out the one who made his master angry.

Get Started! What talents has God given you (serving, singing, telling others about Jesus,..)? _____
Are you using your talents to serve God? ____

TUESDAY
Luke 19:28-40

Train Your Brain: Fill in the blanks with the words the people cried out in verse 38.

"Blessed _____ the _____ who _____ in the name of the _____. Peace in _____ and _____ in the _____."

Get Started! The disciples obeyed Jesus' instructions about the colt even though they did not understand. Circle your attitude about obeying.

NO WAY

I DELAY

RIGHT AWAY

WEDNESDAY
Luke 19:45-48

Complete the sentence by following the maze and writing the letters in the blanks as you come to them.

Jesus says the temple is to be a house of

_ _ _ _ _ _ .

Put prayer to work. Everyone knows someone with problems. Select one adult you know and pray for that person every day this week.

THURSDAY
Luke 20:9-17

If you are a Christian, Jesus should be the most important part of your life. Jesus is the cornerstone, the strongest part of the building. Finish the building by writing on the bricks ways you can grow closer to Jesus.

In this parable, the owner is God, His servants were the prophets, and Jesus was the son of the owner. The story shows how the nation of Israel rejected Christ. Pray for the Jewish people to realize their need for Jesus.

FRIDAY
Luke 20:9-17

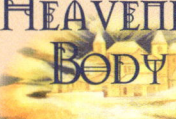

When Christians are resurrected from the dead, they will not have bodies like on earth. Draw a line from the words that describe your heavenly or your earthly body.

- can get married
- can get sick
- cannot die

Body — **Heavenly Body**

- children of the resurrection
- equal to/ like the angels
- can be sad

While on earth you must take care of the body God has given you. List three things you can do to be healthy:
1 _____
2 _____
3 _____

SATURDAY
Luke 21:1-4

Circle the person who gave more.
Rich or **Poor widow**

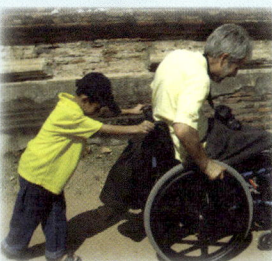

Circle the pictures of things you have given or could do for others.

Comment Corner

WE'RE PROUD OF YOU — stay with it — KEEP TRYING — BE FAITHFUL — you can do it — YOU ARE SPECIAL — keep going — KEEP IT UP — GOD LOVES YOU!

Days Completed

Parent or Leader, circle a comment and/or write your own.

Week 27: Sin's Curse Sent Christ to the Cross

The tomb where Jesus was buried was most likely carved into a large rock. A Large stone was set into a groove and rolled in front of the tomb to keep out thieves or animals.

SUNDAY — Luke 21:5-15

 Use the verses to complete the crossword.

ACROSS
2. What God will give you when you speak (v.15)
4. A sign on earth (v.11)
5. Where people will be taken (v.12)

DOWN
1. The place with beautiful stones and gifts (v.5)
3. _____ will rise up against _____ (v.10)

 Today's verses say that others may not like you just because you are a Christian. Has this ever happened to you? _____ Talk to an adult or older Christian friend about what to do when it happens.

MONDAY — Luke 21:34

 Verse 34 says not to let your heart be weighed down with the worries or cares of this world. Cross out the things that take your heart away from Jesus, and color red the ones that please Jesus.

- sharing
- praying
- fighting
- wasting time on computer or TV
- teasing other kids
- choosing bad friends
- being kind

 If there is an area that you know is not pleasing to Jesus, confess it, and work on it this week.

TUESDAY — Luke 22:1-20

 Answer the questions about today's verses.

Which disciple agreed to betray Jesus? (vv. 3-6) _____

Did Peter and John obey Jesus' instructions for Passover? (vv. 8-13) _____

Who is meant to be remembered in these verses? (vv. 19, 20) _____

On what day was the Passover lamb to be sacrificed? (v. 7) _____

 Ask a parent or adult at church to share with you what communion means to him.

WEDNESDAY
Luke 22:24-27

Use the letters in the box to decode the message from today's verses.

o u t a e

Jes☐s c☐m☐ t☐ s☐rve ☐☐hers, no☐ to be s☐rv☐d.

 Surprise someone at home by helping with a job or chore before you are asked.

THURSDAY
Luke 22:39-46

Prayer will help you to beat temptation. Follow the maze to get away from temptation.

Jesus told His disciples to pray so they would not enter into temptation. What tempts you to sin?
_____
Pray now for God to give you strength to beat this temptation.

FRIDAY
Luke 22:54-62

Under the picture of each rooster, put the number of the verse in which Peter denies Christ.
Write what Peter did in verse 62.
_____

Have you ever denied being a Christian to avoid being teased or picked on? YES NO
Talk to a Christian adult or older Christian friend about how to stand strong for Christ.

SATURDAY
Luke 23:1-12

Find the names from today's verses in the word search.

```
C A E S A R M B F G
T A E A C K D O V A
G A L L H G D P J L
E C T O R F S G R I
M A V P I L A T E L
J E R U S A L E M E
S H E R T O B N C E
H E R O D J E S U S
```

CAESAR
GALILEE
JESUS
PILATE
HEROD
JERUSALEM
CHRIST

The chief priests and crowd were falsely accusing Jesus. Has anyone ever lied about you? YES NO How should you handle it if they do? I should _____

Days Completed

comment corner — WE'RE PROUD OF YOU · stay with it · KEEP TRYING · BE FAITHFUL · you can do it · YOU ARE SPECIAL · keep going · KEEP IT UP · GOD LOVES YOU!

Parent or Leader, circle a comment and/or write your own.

Week 28: God's Gift Gives Life to the Lost

Why do you think there were twelve apostles? Twelve was the number of the tribes of Israel. After Judas took his own life, the apostles chose another man to replace him named Matthias.

SUNDAY
Luke 23:13-25

Train Your Brain: Mark each sentence T for true or F for False.

____ Pilate and Herod both found Jesus guilty. (vv. 14-15)

____ The crowd wanted Jesus released. (v. 18)

____ The crowd wanted Jesus to be crucified. (v. 21)

____ Pilate released Jesus to the crowd. (vv. 24-25)

Get Started! Jesus was not guilty, but the crowd yelled against Him. What will you do the next time you see another child at school being teased or picked on by a group?

_____

MONDAY
Luke 23:32-43

Train Your Brain: Number the events in the correct order.

___ Jesus said, "Father forgive them for they do not know what they are doing."

___ One of the thieves asked Jesus to remember him.

___ Jesus told the thief that he would be in paradise with Him.

___ The soldiers offered Jesus vinegar (sour wine).

___ One of the thieves made fun of Jesus.

___ They divided up Jesus' clothes and cast lots for them.

Get Started! Even at His death, Jesus cared about the thief on the cross. When did you accept Jesus as your personal Savior?

_____

TUESDAY
Luke 23:44-56

Train Your Brain: Match the people to what they said.

"Please let me bury the body of Jesus."

"This was a righteous man."

"Let's get spices to prepare the body of Jesus before the Sabbath."

Joseph

the women of Galilee the

Centurion

Get Started! Write a prayer of thanks for Jesus dying on the cross for you.

_____
_____
_____
_____

WEDNESDAY
Luke 24:1-12

In verse 7 the angels reminded the women what Jesus told them. Write the three things.

1. _____
2. _____
3. _____

Did the apostles believe the women? YES NO
Do you know people who don't believe in Jesus? YES NO
Show them this passage.

FRIDAY
Luke 24:36-40

Believe it or not!
Fill in the blanks of the sentences. All the answers are parts of a person's body.

1. The disciples had doubts in their _____. (v. 38)
2. A spirit or ghost does not have _____ and _____. (v. 39)
3. Jesus shows the disciples His _____ and _____. (v. 40)

A person today cannot physically touch Jesus as the disciples did. How do you know He is really alive today? _____

THURSDAY
Luke 24:13-27

Answer the following questions.

The men were walking to _____
Did the men know that it was Jesus walking with them? _____
How were the men feeling? _____
Who were the men talking about? _____
What did the angels tell the women? _____

Who have you shared the good news of the Gospel with this year? _____

SATURDAY
Luke 24:41-47

What other thing did Jesus do to show that He was alive? (v. 42-43)
Jesus helped the disciples understand what important things from verses 46-48?

1. Christ had to _____.
2. He had to rise from the _____ on the _____ day.
3. Repentance and forgiveness (remission) of _____ should be preached to all _____ beginning with _____.
4. They (the apostles) are _____ of these things.

Practice sharing the message of Christ's death, burial, and resurrection with a Christian friend or family member so you are ready to share it with your unsaved friends.

comment corner — WE'RE PROUD OF YOU · stay with it · KEEP TRYING · BE FAITHFUL · you can do it · YOU ARE SPECIAL · keep going · KEEP IT UP · GOD LOVES YOU!

Days Completed

Parent or Leader, circle a comment and/or write your own.

Week 29 — Four-Faced, Four-Winged Figures with Fancy Wheels

Tattoos were placed on a person's hand or forehead to show that he was a slave. Jewish slaves could also have the name of their master tattooed on their wrist.

SUNDAY
Ezekiel 1:4-14

Ezekiel's Vision

1. How many creatures does Ezekiel see in verse 5? _____
2. How many faces and wings did each creature have in verse 6? _____
3. What are the four faces on the creatures in verse 10? _____

GET STARTED! God had a plan for Ezekiel's life. God has a plan for your life, too. Write down what you feel His plan is for you today. _____

MONDAY
Ezekiel 1:15-21

Fill in the blanks in this sentence.

THE WHEELS WENT WHEREVER THE LIVING CREATURES WENT.

⊛ = H   🔥 = E   ⚡ = I   V = R

GET STARTED! Is it always easy for you to understand God's Word? _____ Write down what you do understand about this passage.

_____
_____
_____

TUESDAY
Ezekiel 2:3-7

Circle the letters that spell the word God uses to describe the Israelites.

W R U E N B O E P L Z L M I W O T U S

GET STARTED! God told Ezekiel to share His Word with the children of Israel whether they listened or not. Do not be discouraged if you share about Jesus with a friend and they do not want to listen. Keep trying.

WEDNESDAY
Ezekiel 3:16-22

God gave Ezekiel a warning to take to the Israelites. Help Ezekiel go through the maze.

Israel

 Do you have a Christian friend who is doing wrong? _____ Tell him in a kind but firm way that God wants him to do right.

THURSDAY
Ezekiel 8: 8-10; 16-18

Use the clues to spell the word below that shows what God hates.

Clue #1 (👁)
Clue #2 (🐦 — BIR)
Clue #3 (🌑 — MON)
Clue #4 (🦁 — ION)
Clue #5 (☀ — UN)

___ ___ ___ ___ ___
#1 #2 #3 #4 #5

 How much time do you spend?
Watching TV _____
Doing your Quiet Time _____
Playing on a computer or game system _____
Doing your homework _____

FRIDAY
Ezekiel 10:2-7

The man was told to scatter coals over Jerusalem to show that the Israelites would be destroyed because of the wicked things they did. Circle the actions below that God would consider wicked.

LYING **STEALING**
Obeying
FIGHTING **Kindness**
THANKFULNESS
Swearing **Bullying**
SELFISHNESS

 Write Yes or No.
_____ Today I acted like a Christian.
_____ Today I talked like a Christian.

SATURDAY
Ezekiel 11:16-21

 Complete the puzzle to find out this truth about God.

1=R, 2=I, 3=P, 4=E, 5=O, 6=S, 7=G, 8=H, 9=M, 10=K, 11=D

ISRAEL →

___ ___ ___   ___ ___ ___ ___ ___
 7 5 11   10 4 4 3   6

___ ___ ___   ___ ___ ___ ___ ___ ___ ___ ___
 8 2 6   3 1 5 9 2 6 4 6

 Write a promise to God on a piece of paper. Put it in an envelope and give it to your parents or leader to keep for one week. After one week, see if you kept your promise to God.

comment corner — WE'RE PROUD OF YOU • stay with it • KEEP TRYING • BE FAITHFUL • you can do it • YOU ARE SPECIAL • keep going • KEEP IT UP • GOD LOVES YOU!

Parent or Leader, circle a comment and/or write your own.

 Days Completed

Week 30

Watch out Judah!

People who worshiped idols often sewed magic charms on their clothing. They believed the charms kept them safe from danger, illness, and evil spirits. (Ezekiel 13:18)

SUNDAY
Ezekiel 12:18-25

JUDGMENT DAY!

The Time Has Come!

Write two words from verse 19 that describe how the people of Israel should eat and drink.

_____ _____

Write two words from verse 20 that describe what will happen to the cities (towns) and land.

_____ _____

Circle the correct answer. According to verse 25 how long will God wait before punishing the Israelites?

Many years from now

Very soon

Never

 Some people doubt that Jesus will one day return in the Rapture to take all the Christians with Him to Heaven. Believe it! He is coming. Are you ready to meet Him today? _____

MONDAY
Ezekiel 13:1-8

WARNING! WARNING!
What group of people was God warning? Follow the trails to place the letters correctly in the word.

 The Bible has everything you need to know about the future. Decide in your heart that you will stay away from games or toys that have anything to do with reading the future or contacting spirits.

TUESDAY
Ezekiel 14:6-11

In the arrow write God's command to His people about what they should do about idols (v. 6).

Write down the three most important people in your life.

_____ _____

_____

Is God on your list?

WEDNESDAY
Ezekiel 14:12-20

Unscramble the names of three Biblical heroes who overcame bad times. Next, unscramble the letters of the word that explains why they were saved (v.14)

OJB   IDLENA   AHON   HOSRTINSEGUSE

___   _____   ____   _____

 These three men chose not to sin even though the rest of their world was living in sin. Choose one of these men to be your hero. Check one.

___ 1. I will be like Noah and do right even if people make fun of me.
___ 2. I will be like Job and do right even if people try to discourage me.
___ 3. I will be like Daniel and do right even when people are unfair to me.

THURSDAY
Ezekiel 18:14-18

After reading this passage, write True or False before each statement.

_____ 1. Godly parents can have wicked children.

_____ 2. Wicked parents can have godly children.

_____ 3. Godly children can break the chain of sin and disobedience in a family.

 Will God believe you when you try to blame another person for your sin? Yes No

FRIDAY
Ezekiel 18:19-20,30

Finish the statement by coloring in the correct letters of the word.

The Lord says that each person will be judged according to his or her

_____

COWNADYUSCT

Even if your parents have made some mistakes, you are still responsible for how you behave and the choices you make. Are you praying for your parents?

SATURDAY
Ezekiel 20:6-16

Answer the questions by choosing the correct letter. Then color in all the correct letters to see what Israel must do.

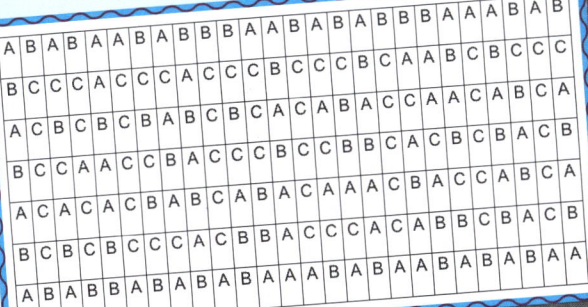

1. **What did God command the children of Israel to turn away from in verse 8?**
   A. Meat   B. Family   C. Idols

2. **What did God give them in verse 12 to show that He is their God and that He made them holy?**
   A. Land   B. Pets   C. Sabbaths

3. **How did God describe the land he wanted to give them in verses 6 and 15?**
   A. a desert place   B. a jungle   C. flowing with milk and honey

Did you disobey a parent or teacher this week? _____ If you did, you also rebelled against God. Ask God and the person to forgive you.

comment corner

WE'RE PROUD OF YOU · stay with it · KEEP TRYING · BE FAITHFUL · you can do it · YOU ARE SPECIAL · keep going · KEEP IT UP · GOD LOVES YOU!

Days Completed

Parent or Leader, circle a comment and/or write your own.

Week 31

Parables and Predictions

In order to tell the future, people would study how to read the liver of an animal. In Ezekiel 21 the king of Babylon reads a liver to help him decide if his plan was a good one.

SUNDAY
Ezekiel 20:17-26

Follow the mazes for the parents and their children.

The Israelite parents disobeyed God. God gave their children another chance.

Did the children learn the lessons God wanted them to learn? (See v. 21)
Yes No

Parents in the Wilderness

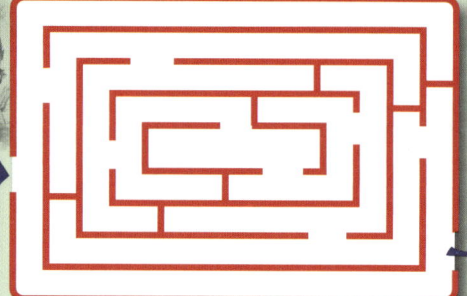

Children in the Wilderness

Write down something that you have learned from your parents this year.
_____

MONDAY
Ezekiel 20:40-44

One day the nation of Israel will remember what they have done to God and themselves. In verse 43, God says that they will **LOATHE** themselves because of all the evil things they have done. Shade in the X's to find out what the word **LOATHES** means.

"We want to be just like the Gentiles."

```
t   s v     a     c v     e   d     f     d
  x   s   x   t   x v c x x x x x s x x x x x
e x     f x s   x   x   d   x t   c x         v
  x a   x   x   s   x e x   v   x t   e     c
v x   s c x   x d   b x v   x a     x         t
t x x x x x v x x x x x     x   f   x x x x
  x       t x   x c   x x s   x   d   x   v   b
a x   f   x   x   t   x c   x v   s x     e   a
  x   a   x v x e     x   d x     t x     c s
  x t     x   x   x   v   x     x f   x x x x
e     b s     c   d       t   v   b     a   f
```

One of the consequences of sin is feeling unhappy or guilty. If you feel this way, ask God to show you if there is any unconfessed sin in your life.

TUESDAY
Ezekiel 22: 23-31

Name three groups of people who were not obedient to God.

(Verse 26) _____
(Verse 27) _____
(Verse 28) _____

In verse 30, God was looking for one person in Judah who would be obedient to Him.

Did He find one? YES   NO

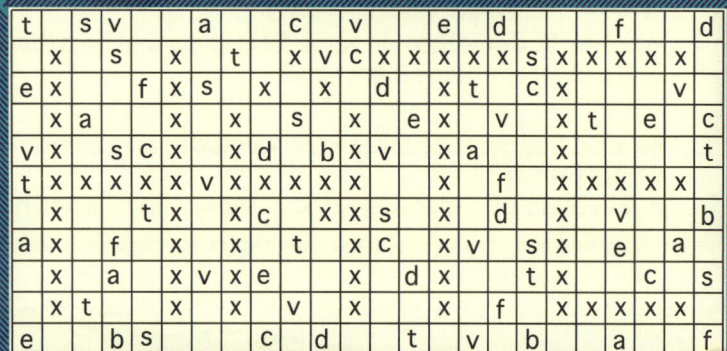

Did you obey your parents yesterday?
Yes   No
How about today?
Yes   No

WEDNESDAY
Ezekiel 26:2-7

Use the following words to complete the sentences. Draw a line from the word to the space. You will use one of the words twice.

_____ was happy that _____ was attacked. _____ said that He would send _____ to destroy _____.

TYRE (TYRUS)   **JERUSALEM**   **GOD**   **NEBUCHADNEZZAR**

Have you made fun of someone this year? Ask God to help you to use your words in a kind not a hurtful way.

THURSDAY
Ezekiel 28:11-17

God created Satan to be a beautiful angel. Satan chose to sin. Color Satan's good characteristics before he sinned green. Color in red the characteristics that caused him to sin.

Wisdom   **PRIDE**   **CORRUPT**   **Beauty**

Satan was a leader in God's heavenly army of angels before he sinned. Satan made one bad choice and lost his position before God. While we cannot lose our salvation by making bad choices, our fellowship with God can be broken. Have you broken your fellowship with God this week because of bad choices you have made? Ask God to forgive you. Spend some time in fellowship with Him.

FRIDAY
Ezekiel 33:1-7

Find the words in the word search.

BLOOD BLOW SOUND SWORD TRUMPET WARNING WATCHMAN

```
Y Z U B L O W L
L W A R N I N G
O Q S O U N D N
W A T C H M A N
A O S W O R D P
R B D O O L B A
T R U M P E T L
```

Ezekiel had the important job of being a watchman. Your job is important, too. How long has it been since you last shared Christ with someone?

SATURDAY
Ezekiel 33:11-20

Is God Fair? Answer Yes or No to each question.

_____ 1. Does God take pleasure in wicked people dying?
_____ 2. Would God rather have the wicked turn away from their sin?
_____ 3. Can righteous people do bad things?
_____ 4. Can wicked people change their ways?
_____ 5. Did the people of Israel complain that the way of the Lord was not equal, right, or just?
_____ 6. Will the Lord judge each person according to his own ways?

Even if your parents are Christians, you may not be one. Write down the age you were when you accepted Jesus as your Savior. If you can't remember doing that, ask a parent or leader to explain it to you.

comment corner

WE'RE PROUD OF YOU   stay with it   KEEP TRYING   BE FAITHFUL   you can do it   YOU ARE SPECIAL   keep going   KEEP IT UP   GOD LOVES YOU!

Days Completed

Parent or Leader, circle a comment and/or write your own.

Week 32
Giving Bodies to Bones

Do you know why sheep were so important to Israel? The sheep gave them wool, meat, and were also used for sacrifices. The shepherd knew each of his sheep by name.

SUNDAY
Ezekiel 33:23-31

The Jews thought they had a right to the land because Abraham had inherited it. Find out what Ezekiel told them. Use the letter of the alphabet that comes after the letter under the spaces to find the missing words. For example: T=U, C=D, H=I.

Abraham was _ _ _ _ _ _ _ _ _
Q H F G S D N T R

but those left in the land were _ _ _ _ _ _ .
V H B J D C

Just because you are a Christian and go to church doesn't mean that you are a righteous person. You must choose to do right. Ask your parents how you are doing in the area of making right choices.

MONDAY
Ezekiel 34:1-6, 11-16

Some sheep were cared for and others were not. Look up the verses on each sheep. If it was taken care of, circle it; if it wasn't, cross it out. Who took good care of the sheep?

_____

Ezekiel 34:2-6

Ezekiel 34:12-16

When God gives you a job to do, you need to do your best. Ask your teachers if they think your schoolwork is showing your best work.

TUESDAY
Ezekiel 34:24-31

In these verses, God's people are the good sheep. Answer the questions to find out more about these promises.

1. What kind of covenant will God make?
   _____ (v. 25)

2. In verse 28, the good sheep will live safely and not be what?
   _____

3. Circle the verse numbers which tell you who owns the sheep.
   26 27 30 31

Is someone bigger and stronger trying to bully you? Pray for that person and talk to your parents or leader about it.

WEDNESDAY
Ezekiel 36:10-15

God promises the nation Israel that they will be fruitful one day. Write down the promises God makes to Israel from the following verses.

VERSE 11
_____
_____
_____

VERSE 15
_____
_____
_____

GET STARTED! You don't know what great plans God has for you. Write requests in your prayer diary that you can pray about now that will affect your future (college, ministry, job, marriage...).

THURSDAY
Ezekiel 36:20-25

TRAIN YOUR BRAIN Israel had profaned (cursed, abused) God's holy what? To find the answer only color the spaces with the letter N.

GET STARTED! Would your friends say that your testimony at school or in your neighborhood brings **shame** or **fame** to God's name. Circle your answer.

FRIDAY
Ezekiel 36:26-32

God will give the Israelites a spiritual makeover. Fill in the missing letters.

BEFORE   AFTER

Verse 26
heart of _ _ _ _ _ _ _

heart of _ _ _ _ _ _ _

Verse 30
F _ _ _ _ _ _ _

Multiply (increase) _ _ _ _ _ _ _ of the trees

GET STARTED! How has your life changed since you asked Jesus into your heart?
_____
_____

SATURDAY
Ezekiel 37:1-14

As a nation, Israel was dead. She had no land, king, or temple. Her people were scattered to other nations. It seemed hopeless that they would ever be united again.

What did God tell Ezekiel to do? Look at verse 4. _____

Draw a picture under the word After to show how the bones changed.

BEFORE   AFTER

GET STARTED! Do you know someone who is going through a hard time? Find a verse from God's Word to encourage him. Share it with him as soon as you can.

comment corner — WE'RE PROUD OF YOU • stay with it • KEEP TRYING BE FAITHFUL • you can do it • YOU ARE SPECIAL • keep going • KEEP IT UP • GOD LOVES YOU!

Parent or Leader, circle a comment and/or write your own.

Days Completed

Week 33 — God Versus Gog

The Dead Sea is six times saltier than the ocean. However, the river that Ezekiel describes will cause the Dead Sea to become completely salt-free.

SUNDAY
Ezekiel 37:19-22

TRAIN YOUR BRAIN: Write the names on the sticks of the tribes that God will join together (v.19).

What was God trying to show the Israelites with the two sticks? (v. 22)

God would make them one _____ on the mountains of _____ and they would have one _____.

GET STARTED! Write the name of an unsaved friend in your prayer diary and pray for him or her.

MONDAY
Ezekiel 38:3-12

TRAIN YOUR BRAIN: God allows Israel to be attacked by Gog. Write the names on each horse of the three other nations that will attack Israel. (v.5)

GET STARTED! The nation of Israel has many enemies even today. Name one.

_____

Pray for Israel and her enemies that they will come to know Christ as Savior.

TUESDAY
Ezekiel 38:18-23

TRAIN YOUR BRAIN: Circle the pictures of the things that will shake or fall down from today's verses.

GET STARTED! God is loving, but He is also just. He will judge wicked people and nations. Pray for your country and her leaders.

Week 34

Live Your Life for the Lord

In Paul's day, Olympic athletes had to prove that they spent at least ten months in training before competing in their sport. The last month of training had to be under an official Olympic instructor.

SUNDAY
Philippians 1:1-6

On the envelope write the names of the people who wrote the letter in the section marked *From*. In the spot marked *To*, write the names of the group to whom it was written. To discover the type of letter that was written, write the letter of the alphabet that comes before the letter listed. One letter is already given to you.

This was a letter of
_____ A _____
U I   O L T H J W J O H

From: _____

To: _____

GET STARTED! Have you written this kind of letter to a person who helps you grow in your faith? Write one today.

MONDAY
Philippians 1:8-14

Because of Paul's examples of courage, Christians were encouraged to be bolder in sharing the Word of God. List two reasons why Christians today are afraid to share the Gospel.

1. _____
2. _____

 Are you afraid to share the Gospel? Pray and ask God to give you the courage to witness to your friends at school.

TUESDAY
Philippians 1:19-21

What is the reason for living? Fill in the missing vowels (a, e, i, o, u) to find Paul's answer.

F_r t_ m_
t_ l_v_ _s
Chr_st _nd
t_ d__ _s
g__n

(v. 21).

 Ask your Olympian leader or Sunday school teacher if you can share your testimony in class.

Week 35

Running the Race for Jesus

While Paul was a prisoner for two years in Rome he was allowed to have visitors. However, guards watched him day and night with one guard handcuffed to Paul at all times.

SUNDAY
Philippians 2:24-30

Draw a line from the man to the phrases that tell what happened to him from these verses.

Paul

Epaphroditus

is being sent to them
God had mercy on him
hopes to come to them soon
sick to the point of death
is sending someone to them

 Make a get-well card for someone who is sick or in the hospital. Write a verse in it to comfort and encourage him.

MONDAY
Philippians 3:1-6

According to verse 2, Paul wants us to beware of what three kinds of people?

BEWARE OF
_____
_____

BEWARE OF
_____
_____

BEWARE OF
_____
_____

 Knowing the truth of God's Word will keep you from believing false teachers. Did you do your Quiet Time faithfully all last week? _____ all last month? _____

TUESDAY
Philippians 3:12-14

The Olympian motto is found in verse 14. Write it on the banner below.

_____
_____
_____
_____
_____
_____

 If you haven't memorized Philippians 3:14 yet, do it today.

WEDNESDAY
Philippians 3:17-21

Write True or False by each statement.

_____ 1. Paul tells them to follow his example.
_____ 2. While Paul is writing, he is laughing.
_____ 3. Paul says that some people are enemies of the cross of Christ.
_____ 4. Our citizenship (or conversation) is on earth.
_____ 5. One day Jesus will change our bodies to be like His glorious body.

 Be an example for others to follow. Others are watching you. Help a younger child learn verses this week.

THURSDAY
Philippians 4:4-7

Paul gives advice to the Philippians just like your mom gives you last minute words of advice as you go to school or out to play. Write in your own words the advice Paul is giving from these verses.

Verse 4: _____
Verse 5: _____
Verse 6: _____

 Write down words of advice your parents often tell you.
_____
_____

FRIDAY
Philippians 4:8-13

Verse 8 tells us to "think on" what eight things?

Impure or "dirty" messages and pictures are everywhere. What is your plan to keep your mind pure?
_____
_____

SATURDAY
Philippians 4:14-19

Giving support to missionaries is very important. Paul was grateful for the gifts the church had given him. Write two ways you can help missionaries.

Kevin & Gretchen Gregory

1. _____
2. _____

Ask your Olympian Club leader or Sunday school teacher for ideas on how you can help a missionary. Do something special for one of your church missionaries. A note to let the missionary know you pray for them is always a blessing.

comment corner — WE'RE PROUD OF YOU • stay with it • KEEP TRYING BE FAITHFUL • you can do it • YOU ARE SPECIAL • keep going • KEEP IT UP • GOD LOVES YOU!

Parent or Leader, circle a comment and/or write your own.

Days Completed

Week 36 — Lessons From the Grapevine

Towers were built in the middle of vineyards and guards would watch for people or animals stealing grapes. The guards would shoot arrows at the thieves.

SUNDAY
Isaiah 1:16-20

STOP DOING WRONG.

LEARN TO DO RIGHT!

Draw a line to the items that go together.

Stop (cease)	To do good (well or right)
Learn	Devoured by the sword
Seek	Justice (judgment)
Plead	For the widow
Scarlet sins	Doing evil (wrong)
Refuse (resist) and rebel	White as snow

GET STARTED! Is there one sin that you keep repeating? YES NO
Confess this sin to God, ask His forgiveness, and ask for His help in overcoming it this week.

MONDAY
Isaiah 4:2-6

1. Circle the words that describe the Branch of the Lord. (v. 2)

   broken   beautiful   glorious   ruined

2. What would God create over Mount Zion by day? _____ (v.5) by night? _____

GET STARTED! Notice God's love and protection as He gives His people a shelter from the sun and safety from the storm. God loves you, too, and He is able to protect you. What are you afraid of?

_____

Realize that God is bigger than whatever you wrote! Thank Him for loving you and protecting you. Ask Him to help you trust Him when you are afraid.

TUESDAY
Isaiah 5:1-7

The Vineyard Song by Isaiah

1. Did the man take good care of his vineyard?
   Yes   No
2. Did the vineyard produce good grapes?
   Yes   No
3. What will the owner of the vineyard do?
   Try again   Leave it alone   Let it be destroyed
4. Whom does the vineyard represent? (v. 7)
   _____

GET STARTED! An important Biblical principle is obedience brings blessing; disobedience brings a curse (punishment). So how was your day yesterday? Blessed   Punished

WEDNESDAY
Isaiah 6:1-8

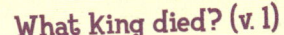

Isaiah's Vision.
Match the correct answer to the questions below.

___ What King died? (v. 1)
___ Where was the Lord seated? (v. 1)
___ How did the seraphim describe God? (v. 3)
___ What did God ask? (v. 8)
___ What did Isaiah answer? (v. 8)

A. Here am I, send me.
B. Holy, holy, holy
C. Uzziah
D. On a throne
E. Whom shall I send?

Isaiah was a willing volunteer. He didn't complain or make excuses. Isaiah's job was not all that fun! Write down one job that you will volunteer to do for your mom or dad this week – without complaining! _____ Don't forget to do it!

THURSDAY
Isaiah 7:10-16

Isaiah tells king Ahaz that God will give him a sign. Unscramble the letters to complete the sentences.

A _____ (riving) will be with child and give birth to a _____ (nso), and will call him _____ (mulemlan).
What is another name for this baby?
_____ (ssJue)

Think about this. Isaiah gave Ahaz the sign of Jesus' birth more than 700 years before Jesus was actually born!
Does God keep His promises? Yes No
Does God know your future? Yes No

FRIDAY
Isaiah 8:11-18

Help Isaiah find the path that leads to God in the maze below.

Don't follow the people, follow me.

Peer pressure means doing something because everyone else is doing it. Write down one example of peer pressure that causes you to struggle. _____
_____
Whom should you follow, your friends or God?
_____
Pray and ask God to help you resist peer pressure this week and to obey His Word.

SATURDAY
Isaiah 9:1-7

Isaiah's warning is judgment followed by a message of hope. God will send them His Son to deliver them. Solve the puzzle below to find some of the names given to God's Son.

A O E I U

W_ND_RF_L C_NS_L_R
M_GHTY G_D _V_RL_ST_NG F_TH_R
PR_NC_ _F P__C_

Do you know a song or chorus that has one of these names in it? Sing it.

comment corner
WE'RE PROUD OF YOU   stay with it   KEEP TRYING   BE FAITHFUL   you can do it   YOU ARE SPECIAL   keep going   KEEP IT UP   GOD LOVES YOU!

Parent or Leader, circle a comment and/or write your own.

Days Completed

Week 37 — The King is Coming!

The ancient city of Babylon is located 55 miles south of Baghdad in Iraq. In 1982 Saddam Hussein had the 85 foot thick walls rebuilt just like they were during the time of King Nebuchanezzar.

SUNDAY
Isaiah 10:20-25

TRAIN YOUR BRAIN

Fill in the blanks using the word bank below.

Word Bank: judgment, return, Israel, anger, remnant, Assyrian, disobedience, rely

God warned _____ that He would judge them because of their _____.
Only a _____ (small leftover part) of Israel would _____ to God and truly _____ on Him.
God would use the _____ army to bring _____ on Israel, but after a short time He would turn His _____ away from Israel and toward the Assyrians.

GET STARTED! Do you obey right away, or do you choose to live your own way? Are you stubborn? **Yes No** Stubbornness against God is SIN! Confess it to God and ask Him to help you obey right away!

MONDAY
Isaiah 11:1-9

TRAIN YOUR BRAIN

Isaiah describes the new future King. What will this King be like? Circle the words that describe Him:

cruel   righteous   wise   wicked   powerful   weak

Even things in nature will be under His control. List two things about nature or the animals that will be different than it is now. (vv. 6-8)

1. _____
2. _____

Who do you think this new King is?
_____

GET STARTED! Did you know that Jesus is coming again? The first time He came as a baby in a manger in Bethlehem. But when He comes again He will come as he King of kings, and will declare war on Satan and his followers, and Jesus will win! Are you ready to meet your new King? **YES NO**

TUESDAY
Isaiah 12:1-6

TRAIN YOUR BRAIN

Finish this verse by unscrambling the words.

God is my
_____
NSOAVLATI
I will
_____
TUSRT
and not be
_____
AAFDIR

GET STARTED! Underline Isaiah 12:2 in your bible and memorize it. This verse will help you when you are afraid.

WEDNESDAY
Isaiah 13:9-13

 "The day of the Lord" is a future time when Jesus will come back to judge this world. Find the judgment words in the puzzle.

DESTROY
DARK
ANGER
PUNISH
CRUEL
TREMBLE

```
D A D C R U E N
T R E M B L E T
P A S B L E N G
U H T I N U A L
N C R U E L N G
I A O Y L N G R
S R Y M B L E D
H R E M D A R K
```

 Do you want to be living on the earth during this time of judgment? **Yes No** If you have trusted Christ as your Savior, you will already be in heaven before this day of the Lord comes. Thank you, God!

THURSDAY
Isaiah 14:12-17

 How many times do you see the words "I will" in verses 13 and 14? _____

Unscramble the letters to find the sin problem:
DERPI _____
What is the middle letter of this word? ____

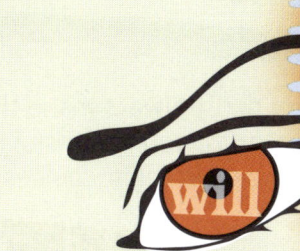

Do you have an "I" problem? Write down one way you have been proud this week.
_____
_____
Ask God to help you have a humble heart.

FRIDAY
Isaiah 25:1-9

Fill in the missing words.

1. "O Lord, you are _____ God." (v. 1)
2. What does God do for the poor and needy? (v. 4) _____
3. What will God prepare for all people? (v. 6) _____
4. What will God wipe away? (v. 8) _____

 Is the God who created the universe your God? **Yes No**
Have you trusted in Jesus as your Savior? **Yes No**
Are you allowing Him to be the Lord (Ruler, Master) of your life? **Yes No**

SATURDAY
Isaiah 26:1-6

1. Who is allowed to enter into the strong city? (v. 2) _____
2. What will you have if you keep your mind on God? (v. 3) _____
3. How long should we trust God? (v. 4) _____
4. What will God do to the proud and lofty? (v. 5) _____

Write down one time when you or your family trusted God for help or protection.
_____
_____

comment corner — WE'RE PROUD OF YOU • stay with it • KEEP TRYING • BE FAITHFUL • you can do it • YOU ARE SPECIAL • keep going • KEEP IT UP • GOD LOVES YOU!
Parent or Leader, circle a comment and/or write your own.

Days Completed

Week 38 — From Punishment to Peace

One method of threshing was to have a donkey pull a wooden sledge over the grain. The sledge had wheels on it to make the ride easier on the driver as he rode on it. (Isaiah 28:28)

SUNDAY
Isaiah 28:1-13

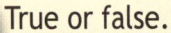

True or false.

_____ The prophets of Israel were setting a good example for the Jewish people.

_____ The priests and prophets of Israel were drunk with wine and beer (strong drink).

_____ God ignored their sin and did nothing about it.

_____ God wanted to give them rest and peace, but they would not listen to Him.

_____ God judged their sin.

 All people in important positions of leadership don't always make the right choices — the leaders of Israel sure didn't. Pray right now for your pastor(s) or club leaders and ask God to give them a pure heart and help them to make right choices every day.

MONDAY
Isaiah 28:23-29

Put the following farm jobs in order from first (1) to last (5).

___ Harvest (pick) the grain
___ Break up (plow) the soil.
___ Level the ground
___ Grind the grain to make bread
___ Plant (sow) the seed

 Just as a farmer knows what he needs to do to grow his crops, God also knows what He needs to do to cause His children to grow spiritually, and it's not always comfortable for you and me. What hard time has God used in your life to cause you to grow closer to Him?

_____

TUESDAY
Isaiah 29:13-16

Read verse 13 again, then write the words **near** and **far** under the correct picture.

 GOD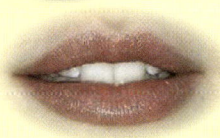

_____   _____

In verse 16, who is the Potter?
_____

Who is the clay? _____
What did the clay say about the Potter?
_____
_____

 Israel could say all the right things, but their hearts were far from God. Is your relationship with God just talk? **Yes   No**
What kind of clay are you?
Happy   Complaining

WEDNESDAY
Isaiah 30:9-12,15-18

Write **I** if the word describes Israel or **G** if it describes God.

____ Rebellious, deceitful (lying) children (v. 9)
____ Don't tell me what is right! (v. 10)
____ Wants to be gracious and compassionate (v. 18)
____ Blesses those who wait for Him (v. 18)
____ Rejected Isaiah's message (v. 12)

GET STARTED!
Are you unwilling to listen to God's instruction? Yes No
Does God enjoy disciplining you when you rebel against Him? Yes No
Circle the one that you would choose: **Obedience and blessing**   **Disobedience and discipline**

THURSDAY
Isaiah 32:13-20

What happens in verse 15 that brings a change in Israel?
_____

Draw a line from the words that describes Israel BEFORE or AFTER the Spirit's coming.

BEFORE   DESERTED   **AFTER**
FRUITFUL
ABANDONED
PEACEFUL
QUIET
THORNS AND BRIARS

GET STARTED!
If you are a Christian, you have the Holy Spirit living inside of you! You should be able to see a change in your life. Write a word to describe you *before* and *after* you became a Christian. If you are not sure, ask your parents or pastor.

FRIDAY
Isaiah 33:17-22

At a time still future God will destroy all of Israel's enemies. The Lord is described by three names in verse 22. Write these names on the lines below the pictures.

_____   _____   _____

GET STARTED!
God is the King of kings, but His home right now is in Heaven. Who is the leader of your country?
_____
Pray for him today, that he will fear and obey God.

SATURDAY
Isaiah 35:3-10

Use the clues below to complete the crossword puzzle.

1. The highway will be called the Way of _____. (v.8)
2. The eyes of the Blind will be _____. (v.5)
3. Only the _____ will walk there. (v.9)
4. What will the lame man do? (v.6)
5. The dry ground will become a _____. (v.7)

GET STARTED!
Sing a song of praise to God right now for all that He has done for you. What song did you choose? _____

comment corner — WE'RE PROUD OF YOU · stay with it · KEEP TRYING · BE FAITHFUL · you can do it · YOU ARE SPECIAL · keep going · KEEP IT UP · GOD LOVES YOU!   **Days Completed**
Parent or Leader, circle a comment and/or write your own.

Week 39
The Lord Is the Lover of Lambs

To separate the grain from the husks, the Israelites would put pieces of metal or stone in a log and drag it over the grain. After that, they would throw it into the air and let the wind blow away the outside husk.

SUNDAY
Isaiah 40:6-11

Write your answers

1. People are described as what in verse 6? _____
2. What lasts forever in verse 8? _____
3. What is God like in verse 11? _____
4. Circle all the things a shepherd does for his sheep.

- Protects them
- Feeds them
- Helps them when they're hurt
- Leads them
- Gives them places to rest

Get Started! Write down one example of how God takes care of you: _____ Thank Him for taking care of you.

MONDAY
Isaiah 40:28-31

Circle the words that describe God.

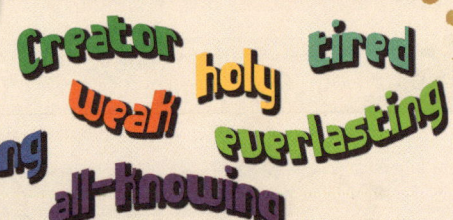

Creator, tired, weak, holy, everlasting, strong, all-knowing

Write out verse 31:
_____
_____
_____
_____
_____

Get Started! Underline in your Bible and memorize Isaiah 40:31. This verse can help you the next time you need strength to keep going!

TUESDAY
Isaiah 41:9-14

Solve the puzzle to find out the message God wants Israel to know.

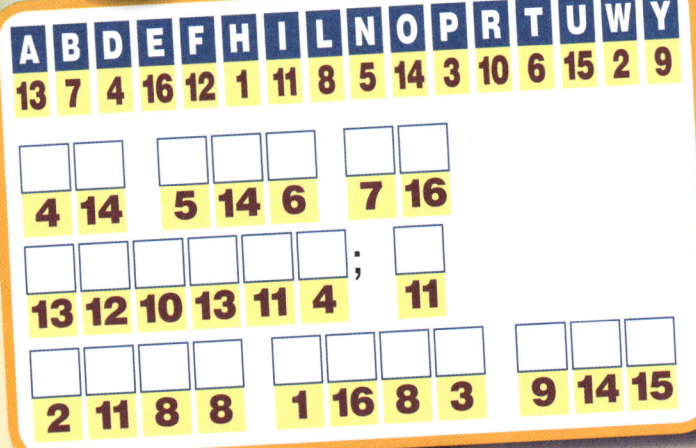

A	B	D	E	F	H	I	L	N	O	P	R	T	U	W	Y
13	7	4	16	12	1	11	8	5	14	3	10	6	15	2	9

☐ ☐ ☐ ☐ ☐ ☐ ☐
4 14   5 14 6   7 16

☐ ☐ ☐ ☐ ☐ ☐ ; ☐
13 12 10 13 11 4   11

☐ ☐ ☐ ☐ ☐ ☐ ☐ ☐ ☐ ☐ ☐
2 11 8 8   1 16 8 3   9 14 15

Get Started! Which of your fears have you given to God?
None   Some   All

WEDNESDAY
Isaiah 42:5-9

TRAIN YOUR BRAIN — Write the word on the colored line that matches the colored boxes.

light | called | earth | hand | created | breath | covenant

God _____ the heavens and the _____. He gives _____ to the people. To the Israelites He says, "I _____ you in righteousness; I will hold your _____ and make you a _____ for the people and a _____ to the Gentiles."

GET STARTED! Just as God had a plan for the Israelites, He has a good plan for you. What do you want to be when you grow up? _____ If God has a different plan for you, are you willing to change yours? _____

THURSDAY
Isaiah 43:4-11

TRAIN YOUR BRAIN — The nation of Israel rejects God as their Savior. God never changed how He feels about them. Write in your own words how God feels about Israel from these verses.

Verse 4 _____
Verse 10 _____
Verse 11 _____

GET STARTED! Pray for the nation of Israel.

FRIDAY
Isaiah 43:14-15, 20-23

TRAIN YOUR BRAIN — Write down four names that God uses to refer to Himself in verse 15.

_____
_____
_____
_____

Who honors God? (v. 20) _____
Who are God's chosen people? _____
Who did not honor God? (v. 23) _____

GET STARTED! Why do you think Israel got tired of God? _____
Could the same thing happen to you? Yes No
Keep faithful to reading your Bible and praying.

SATURDAY
Isaiah 44:6-8, 21-24

TRAIN YOUR BRAIN — Find the underlined words in the puzzle. God said, "I am the <u>first</u> and I am the <u>last</u>; apart from <u>Me</u> there is no God." God wanted <u>Israel</u> to <u>remember</u> who He is, and to <u>return</u> because He had <u>redeemed</u> her.

MEERRMEB
RRNUTE   LATS
IRSELA   TIFSR

_ _ D _ _ _ _ D

GET STARTED! If you are a Christian, Christ has redeemed you. Psalm 107:2 says "Let the redeemed of the Lord say so!" With whom have you shared the Gospel? _____

comment corner
WE'RE PROUD OF YOU · stay with it · KEEP TRYING · BE FAITHFUL · you can do it · YOU ARE SPECIAL · keep going · KEEP IT UP · GOD LOVES YOU!

Parent or Leader, circle a comment and/or write your own.

Days Completed

Week 40

What Titles Do You Give Your Idols?

The nation of Israel was often involved in idol worship. Some idol worshippers did human sacrifice as they worshipped a large statue of a fly known as Baal-Zebub (2 Kings 1:2; 2 Kings 21:6).

SUNDAY
Isaiah 45:5-13

Use the word bank to complete the blanks below:

| Know | No | Created | Arguing |

I am the Lord and there is _____ other god beside me. (v. 5)
God helped Israel so that His people would _____ that there is no other god. (v. 6)
Isaiah warned Israel against _____ with God. (vv. 9-10)
Isaiah says over and over again that God _____ the earth and everything in it. (v. 12)

GET STARTED! Put a check next to the things about you that God controls.
☐ skin color ☐ eye color ☐ parents ☐ brothers/sisters ☐ where you were born

Have you ever complained about the way God made you? Yes No
Is God pleased with your complaining? Yes No

MONDAY
Isaiah 45:5-13

God created the heavens and the earth.
What is an idol? _____
_____
_____

Can an idol save anyone? _____
Who alone can save? _____
We know that God wants to save Israel. Who else is He willing to save? (v. 22)
_____

GET STARTED! Write down three idols that people have today.
1. _____
2. _____
3. _____

Circle one that is the biggest temptation for you. Ask God to help you keep Him first in your life.

TUESDAY
Isaiah 46:6-9

Idol Talk
What were idols made of?
_____ _____
What did the people do after the idol was made?
_____
How is an idol described in verses 6-7? _____
   A. Cannot move   B. Does not answer
   C. Cannot save   D. All of the above

Write down from verse 9 what God wants Israel to remember.
_____
_____
_____

GET STARTED! Write down a time when God has helped you or your family in the past. What problems can you trust God with today?

Past _____
_____
_____

Today _____
_____
_____

94

WEDNESDAY
Isaiah 48:1-7

TRAIN YOUR BRAIN

Unscramble the words to complete God's message to Israel

> I warned you, Israel, that this would happen from long ago, but you would not _____ (nestil) because you are _____ (bornstub). You cannot blame your _____ (slodi) for doing this. Now I will tell you _____ (ewn) things that you have _____ (reevn) heard before.

GET STARTED!

Are you stubborn? **Yes No**
Which is always better, *your way* or *God's way*? (Circle one)
You can learn from Israel's example, or you can learn the hard way. Confess any stubbornness to God and ask Him to soften your heart and help you submit to His will.

THURSDAY
Isaiah 48:17-22

TRAIN YOUR BRAIN

1. What are three names for God in verse 17?
   _____
   _____
   _____

2. What would Israel have enjoyed if she had followed God's commands? (vv. 18-19)
   A. Peace (well-being)   B. Righteousness
   C. Many descendants   D. All the above

3. What is the good news at the end of verse 20?
   _____

4. What do the wicked not have? (v. 22)
   _____

GET STARTED!

God wanted to bless Israel, but He couldn't because of her rebellious heart. Is there sin in your life that might stop God from blessing you?

FRIDAY
Isaiah 49:8-13

Israel's past deliverance from the Babylonians is a picture of Israel's future deliverance when the Lord returns to be Israel's King. Circle the words that describe this future deliverance.

> freedom   comfort
> help   hunger
> safety   thirst   fear
> compassion   joy
> singing

Write down one way God has helped you.
_____
_____

SATURDAY
Isaiah 49:22-23

TRAIN YOUR BRAIN

Break the code to find a beautiful promise from verse 23.

9	4	3	7	2	1	8	5	6
disappointed	in	hope	not	who	Those	be	God	will

Boxes: 1, 2, 3, 4, 5, 6, 7, 8, 9

GET STARTED!

Circle the items that you trust in today.
friends   family   money   fun   sports   good grades   popularity   good looks

All of the above will disappoint you someday. If you don't want to be disappointed, where should your hope or trust be? _____

---

comment corner — WE'RE PROUD OF YOU | stay with it | KEEP TRYING BE FAITHFUL | you can do it | YOU ARE SPECIAL | keep going | KEEP IT UP | GOD LOVES YOU!

Parent or Leader, circle a comment and/or write your own.

Days Completed

Week 41 — His Pain—Our Gain

Many people believed in an ancient myth of a creature named Rahab who tried to stop God from creating the world. Rahab was also the name the Israelites gave to Egypt. (Isaiah 51:9)

SUNDAY
Isaiah 50:4-9

God's Servant

This servant was not _____. (v. 5)

List three ways this servant was mistreated. (v.6)
_____ _____ _____

Whom does this servant rely on for help? (v. 7)
_____

Who might this servant be? (for help look up Matt. 27:27-31)
_____

GET STARTED! God's people can suffer for their faith. Write one person whom you know has suffered for his or her faith in Christ.
_____

MONDAY
Isaiah 51:4-8

God comforts His people with the promise of His coming salvation.

What are His first three or four words in verse 4?
_____

What three things will pass away? (v. 6)
_____

What two things will last forever? (vv. 6, 8)
_____

They should not be afraid of what? (v. 7)
_____

 Heaven  Earth People

GET STARTED! Has anyone ever made fun of you because you believe in Jesus? Yes No
How did (would) you feel? _____
How could you encourage someone else who was made fun of? _____

TUESDAY
Isaiah 52:7-10

How exciting it will be when the Lord returns and delivers Israel from her enemies and becomes her King. Find the following words in the puzzle.

```
E G O O D N E S S
C Y X C J O P E I
C O M F O R T I N
R L P Q Y A M X G
F B W I M R O P I
S A L V A T I O N
E F Q A B R S L G
B O P E A C E M P
```

Peace   Joy
Salvation   Goodness
Singing   Comfort

GET STARTED!
Are you looking forward to Heaven?
Yes No
What are you looking forward to seeing or doing in Heaven?
_____

WEDNESDAY
Isaiah 53:1-10

Just think, these verses were written over 700 years before Jesus was even born! Label the following statements True or False.

_____ Jesus was good-looking and everyone liked Him. (vv. 2-3).
_____ Jesus was beaten and died so that we could have peace and life. (v. 5)
_____ We are like sheep who have wandered away from our Shepherd (v. 6)
_____ When Jesus was falsely accused, He argued with the judge. (v. 7)
_____ It was God's will that Jesus should die for the sins of others. (v. 10)

GET STARTED! Do you see the awesome love that God has for you? Take a few minutes to think about how Jesus suffered willingly for you, and thank Him for loving you so much!

THURSDAY
Isaiah 54:4-10

Fill in the blanks with the correct words.

love   afraid   covenant   kindness   little   back

The Lord says to Israel, "Do not be _____. Though I was angry with you for a _____ while, yet I will bring you _____ to Myself and show you _____ and mercy. My _____ for you will never be shaken, and my _____ of peace will never be removed."

GET STARTED! God still loved Israel even though He had to punish her for her rebellion. Does God still love you when you sin against Him? **Yes   No**
What do you need to do after you have sinned? (for help look up 1 John 1:9)
_____
_____

FRIDAY
Isaiah 55:8-12

Match the pictures with the words God compares to them.

1. My thoughts are not your thoughts. My ways are not your ways.
2. My word which goes forth from My mouth.
3. The joy of the people.

GET STARTED! God often uses word pictures to explain His Word. What picture comes to mind when you think about God's love for you? _____

SATURDAY
Isaiah 57:15-21

Draw a line from each statement to the heart it describes. Circle the heart that God wants you to have.

- God will heal and comfort
- Pleases God
- God will punish
- Sorry about its sin
- Makes God angry
- Doesn't care about its sin

BROKEN   **HARD**

GET STARTED! What kind of heart does God want you to have when you sin? **Hard   Broken**
Pray and ask God to break your heart and help you overcome your habit of sin.

comment corner

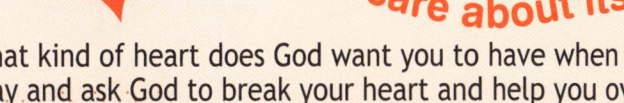

stay with it • WE'RE PROUD OF YOU • KEEP TRYING • BE FAITHFUL • you can do it • YOU ARE SPECIAL • keep going • KEEP IT UP • GOD LOVES YOU!

Parent or Leader, circle a comment and/or write your own.

Days Completed

Week 42

Matters of the Heart

Ancient cities built tall thick walls with many large gates. During the day the gates were open, but at night they were closed to keep out enemies and thieves.

SUNDAY
Isaiah 58:3-9

 **Fasting or Fighting?**

1. What was Israel's problem? (vv. 3-5) _____
   a. They did not know how to fast.
   b. They did not want to fast.
   c. They were fasting and fighting.

2. What did God want Israel to do when they fasted? (vv. 6-7) _____
   a. fight and argue
   b. wear sackcloth and ashes
   c. set the oppressed free and share food with the hungry

3. If Israel had the right heart attitude, what would God's response have been? (vv. 8-9)
   a. I will hear and answer you.
   b. I will help you.
   c. All of the above

4. Which is more important to God, outward actions or heart attitude?
   _____

 Circle all of the following that you do:
Go to church   Pray   Read the Bible   Give money to church   Memorize verses   Share the Gospel with unsaved people.
Why do you do these things? _____

MONDAY
Isaiah 59:1-2

 Israel is wondering why God is not coming to their rescue. Solve the puzzle to find the cause of Israel's trouble.

THE CODE C 11   D 5   F 8   G 14   H 4   M 9   N 3
P 10   R 2   S 12   T 7   V 1   Y 6

 Often we blame God for trouble in our lives when the fault is really our own sinfulness. Write down one example of a time when your sin brought you trouble.
_____

TUESDAY
Isaiah 60:1-6

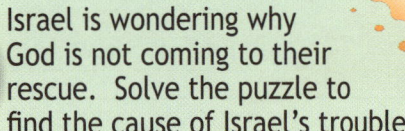 At a time still future, God will reveal His glory through His chosen people Israel, and all the nations of the world will come to see her splendor. Help the nations bring their gifts to Israel in the maze.

 Do you know any Jewish people? **Yes   No** Pray for them today and ask God to open their hearts to the good news of Jesus.

WEDNESDAY
Isaiah 60:19–61:3

1. Why will Israel no longer need the sun and moon? (v. 19) _____
2. What did God want Israel to do? (v. 1)
   To preach (bring) _____
   To bind up (heal) _____
   To proclaim _____
3. What three things did God give to His people? (v. 3)
   _____
   _____
   _____

GET STARTED! Do you like to hear good news? If you are a believer in Christ, then share the good news with someone this week.

THURSDAY
Isaiah 61:7-11

1. How much joy will Israel get? (v.7) _____
2. What does God love? _____
   What does He hate? (v.8) _____
3. God will make what two things spring up before all nations? (v.11)
   _____ and _____

GET STARTED! Pray for the people on your Thursday prayer request page. You may also want to update your answers to prayer.

FRIDAY
Isaiah 65:17-20, 24-25

God will create a new _____ and a new _____ (v.17).

Cross out the things that will not be there and circle the things that will be there.

- Rejoicing
- Crying
- Dying babies
- Wolf and lamb together
- Meat-eating lion
- God's blessing

GET STARTED! Have you accepted Christ as your Savior? Yes No
Are all the members of your family Christians? Yes No

SATURDAY
Isaiah 66:12,13

God will comfort Israel like a what? Color in the dotted sections of the puzzle.

GET STARTED! How does your mom take care of you? _____
God loves you even more than your mom, and He will always care about you.

Comment Corner: WE'RE PROUD OF YOU · stay with it · KEEP TRYING · BE FAITHFUL · you can do it · YOU ARE SPECIAL · keep going · KEEP IT UP · GOD LOVES YOU!

Days Completed

Parent or Leader, circle a comment and/or write your own.

Week 43

The Loyal Love of the Lord

It was the custom to sing the Psalms during Passover. At the Last Supper, Jesus and His disciples probably sang Psalms 115–118 or Psalms 113–114.

SUNDAY
Psalm 114:1-8

TRAIN YOUR BRAIN

The God of Jacob delivered His chosen people, the Israelites, from Egypt.

1. What miracle did God do to both the Red Sea and the Jordan River so the Israelites could cross?
   _____
   _____

2. Why should the earth tremble in the presence of the Lord?
   - Because God is mean and scary
   - Because God likes to destroy things
   - Because God is all-powerful

GET STARTED! Do you sometimes forget about how mighty your God is? Sing a chorus like **My God is so Big** or **My God is an Awesome God** to remind you of His great power.

MONDAY
Psalm 115:1-11

TRAIN YOUR BRAIN

Write what idols can't do.

can't _____
can't _____
can't _____

can't _____
can't _____
can't _____
can't _____

GET STARTED! The same four words are repeated in verses 9, 10, and 11. Write these words and remember to follow them yourself.

_____ _____
_____ _____

TUESDAY
Psalm 116:1-7

TRAIN YOUR BRAIN

True or False.

_____ 1. God didn't listen to the psalmist.

_____ 2. The psalmist almost died.

_____ 3. The psalmist felt that everyone lied to him.

_____ 4. The psalmist didn't show his thankfulness to God.

GET STARTED! You may know someone who is very sick or going through a very difficult time in their life. Which one of these verses could you share with that person?

Verse _____

100

WEDNESDAY
Psalm 116:15–117:2

1. What is precious to God? (v. 15) _____
2. What phrase is repeated in 116:19 and 117:1-2? _____
3. Why should we praise God? (117:2) _____

GET STARTED!
Death is precious to God. It is when God brings His children home to live with Him forever! If you have trusted Christ as your Savior, when you die you will go to heaven to live with God forever. Are you afraid of death? **Yes   No**

Talk to your parents or Olympian leaders about any fears you might have about death.

THURSDAY
Psalm 118:1-6

Sing it again!
Often in songs a certain phrase is repeated. Write the phrase that is repeated in the first four verses of this psalm.

_____
_____
_____

GET STARTED!
Write down one problem (big or small) that you are facing in your life right now.

_____
_____

Read verse 6 again. Has this verse changed the way you think about your problem?

FRIDAY
Psalm 118:24-29

Solve the puzzle.

Heart puzzle words:
- 3 to
- 9 good
- 5 Lord
- 8 is
- 2 thanks
- 4 the
- 1 Give
- 7 He
- 6 for

1 ___ 2 ___ 3 ___ 4 ___ 5 ___
6 ___ 7 ___ 8 ___ 9 ___

GET STARTED!
A thankful heart is a happy heart! Write down three things that you can be thankful for today.

1. _____
2. _____
3. _____

Now thank God for each item you wrote.

SATURDAY
Psalm 119:1-8

Circle the best word to complete the sentences below.

1. God expects us to (obey / ignore) His precepts and laws. (v. 4)
2. Those who obey God are (blessed / poor). (vv. 1–2)
3. The psalmist wished that he obeyed God (more / less). (v. 5)
4. The psalmist decided that he (will / will not) obey God. (v. 8)

GET STARTED!
How would you rate yourself on this obedience scale? (Circle one number)

Never obey   1   2   3   4   5   **Always obey**

Now ask a parent to rate you. What number did they pick? _____
Ask God to help you obey Him today, in big things and in little things.

comment corner
WE'RE PROUD OF YOU · stay with it · KEEP TRYING · BE FAITHFUL · you can do it · YOU ARE SPECIAL · keep going · KEEP IT UP · GOD LOVES YOU!

Parent or Leader, circle a comment and/or write your own.

Days Completed

Week 44

God's Word—My Delight

The Hebrew alphabet has 22 letters. Some psalms were written in an acrostic form with the first letter of each line starting with a Hebrew letter.

SUNDAY
Psalm 119:9-16

Use the words from the word bank.

FORGET (NEGLECT)   MEDITATE   SIN   REJOICE

Memorizing God's Word will help me not to _____. (v. 11)

I should _____ in following God's directions. (v. 14)

I should _____ on God's precepts (commands). (v. 15)

I will not _____ God's Word. (v. 16)

GET STARTED! What does the word meditate mean? _____
Underline and memorize Psalm 119:11. You'll be glad you did!

MONDAY
Psalm 119:17-24

Find seven synonyms for God's Word hidden in the word search.

```
N P S T A T U T E S
S T N E M G D U J T
C Y M S R Q L P L N
U O N T J J K R Y E
O J M I Q U O E X M
S T L M L M Q C C D
F T D O A A O E R N
V W L N W N B P U A
V I L I C W D T J M
X Z V E G N U S T M
R T Q S R S I A L O
A D U S J O K R P C
```

COMMANDMENTS COMMANDS JUDGMENTS
LAW PRECEPTS STATUTES TESTIMONIES

GET STARTED! Were you excited to do your Quiet Time today? **YES NO**
Write down something you really like to do, something you delight in.

_____

Now compare that with God's Word. Would you rather spend time doing what you wrote above or reading God's Word? Ask God to help you delight in His Word.

TUESDAY
Psalm 119:25-32

Choices, choices, choices! Help this Christian find and choose the way of truth.

Be Selfish

GET STARTED! You make choices every day to either please God or please yourself. Below are some choices that would please God. Check one that you need to work on this week.

___ Choose godly friends   ___ Obey parents
___ Tell the truth   ___ Show love to others
___ Have a good attitude   ___ Use kind words

God doesn't force you to obey Him; He lets you choose. Will you choose God's way or your own?

102

WEDNESDAY
Psalm 119:33-40

Draw a line from the beginning statement to the correct ending.

- (v. 33) Teach me to—   — toward Your testimonies (statutes).
- (v. 34) I will obey your law— — are good.
- (v. 35) I delight in—   — with all my heart.
- (v. 36) Turn my heart—   — follow Your rules.
- (v. 37) Turn my eyes—   — Your commands.
- (v. 39) Your laws—   — away from worthless things (vanity).

 One of God's commands in the Bible is for children to obey their parents. Why is this command good?
_____
Obey your parents quickly and happily this week.

THURSDAY
Psalm 119:41-48

Find the missing words.

1. I _____ in Your Word. (v. 42)
2. I will _____ your law. (v. 44)
3. I will walk in _____. (v. 45)
4. I will speak of your testimonies (statutes) before _____. (v. 46)
5. I love your _____. (vv. 47-48)

Have you ever been made fun of because you are a Christian? Yes No
Read verses 41-42 again. Who loves you even when others are mean?
_____

Was God's Word important to the psalmist?
Yes No
Is God's Word important to you?
Yes No

FRIDAY
Psalm 119:49-56

Answer the following questions.

1. What was the psalmist's comfort in times of suffering? (v. 50) _____
2. What did he do when others made fun of him? (v. 51) _____
3. What did he sing about? (v. 54) _____
4. What did he do at night? (v. 55) _____
5. What did he do all the time? (v. 56) _____

SATURDAY
Psalm 119:57-64

Circle the correct word to complete the sentences.

1. I seek you with (part of / all) my heart. (v. 58)
2. I was (slow / quick) to obey your commands. (v. 60)
3. At midnight I (sleep / give thanks). (v. 62)
4. I am a (friend / enemy) of those who follow you. (v. 63)
5. The earth is (full / empty) of your love and mercy. (v. 64)

Write down three qualities you look for in a good friend.
1. _____ 2. _____ 3. _____
Is it important for you to have friends who want to follow and obey God? Yes No

comment corner
WE'RE PROUD OF YOU | stay with it | KEEP TRYING BE FAITHFUL | you can do it | YOU ARE SPECIAL | keep going | KEEP IT UP | GOD LOVES YOU!

Parent or Leader, circle a comment and/or write your own.

Days Completed

Week 45 — God's Word—My Light

What did people use for light since they didn't have candles in ancient Bible times? They either used a seven stemmed menorah which had a small cup on each stem that held olive oil and a wick or a common lamp made of clay.

SUNDAY
Psalm 119:65-72

 **An Afflicton Makeover**

* Afflicted means being in pain, suffering, or having trouble.

Write how the psalmist acted before and after his affliction. (v. 67)

BEFORE **AFTER**

_____   _____

He said that it was _____ that he was afflicted because he learned what? (v.71)

_____

 Write down a lesson you have learned this year.

_____

MONDAY
Psalm 119:73-80

Break the code to find an important truth from today's verses.

```
 4  9  3  7 11  1 10  5  8  2  6
 A  D  E  F  G  H  M  N  O  R  S
```

```
11  8  9  6       1  4  5  9  6
10  4  9  3      10  3       4  5  9
                              10  3
 7  8  2 10  3    9       3
```

 Is there anything about yourself that you wish you could change?

_____

Who made you?

_____

Does God make any mistakes?
Yes   No

Instead of wanting to change something about yourself, thank God for making you according to His plan and ask Him to use you for His glory.

TUESDAY
Psalm 119:81-88

Time to Wait

1. How does the psalmist feel? He is
   _____
   a. having fun   b. sleeping
   c. hurting   d. giving up

2. When his enemies persecute him, what does the psalmist do?
   _____
   a. spits at them
   b. calls the police
   c. tries to hurt them back
   d. remembers God's commands and promises

3. In what does the psalmist hope or wait? (v. 81)
   _____
   _____

 Have you ever had to wait for God's answer to your prayers? **Yes No**
When God asks us to wait, it just means that His plan is different than our plan, and His plan is always better!

104

WEDNESDAY
Psalm 119:89-96

Not Shaky or Changing but Firm for All Time
Color in the sections that show the words that fit this description.

Choose one of the verses from this passage to underline in your Bible that will help you to stay firm in your faith. Which verse did you choose?
Psalm 119: _____

THURSDAY
Psalm 119:97-104

Help this bee find his way from the flowers back to his beehive.

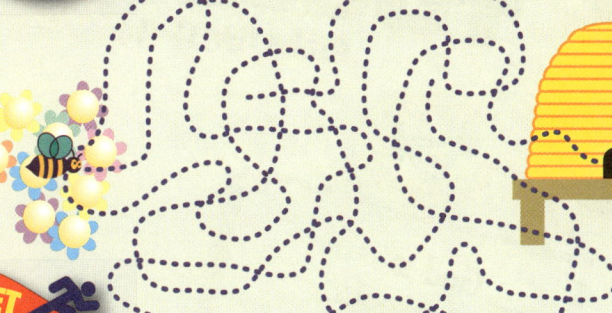

God's Word is sweeter than _____! (v. 103) Is your time in God's Word sweet and satisfying or stale and boring? Make your time with God sweeter by asking Him to help you understand and apply His Word to your life.

FRIDAY
Psalm 119:105-112

Circle all the times that the psalmist has chosen to obey God's Word.

in suffering   in victory
on bad days   on good days   until the end of his life

Write out Psalm 119:105.

_____
_____
_____
_____

Have you ever hiked through the woods at night? Yes No
What would happen if you turned off your flashlight and hiked in the dark? _____
God's Word is our Light, showing us how to follow God's ways and helping us to avoid the dangerous paths in this dark world. What will happen if you do not take the time to read and study God's Word? _____

SATURDAY
Psalm 119:113-120

F. feeling **E.** either **A.** awe or **R.** respect OF THE LORD

1. What does the psalmist love? (v. 113) _____
2. The psalmist says that God is his _____ and _____. (v. 114)
3. Who did the psalmist fear? (v. 120) _____

What does it mean to fear God? _____
Put a check next to the examples that show the fear of God.
☐ Ashley tells her dad that she broke the glass by accident and says she is sorry.
☐ Kayla takes cookies from the cookie jar when her mom is not looking because she is really hungry.
☐ Ryan looks at his neighbor's spelling test because he didn't have time to study.
☐ Brandon tells his friends he doesn't want to watch the movie because it has bad language.
Do you think that the world today fears God? Yes No   Do you fear God? Yes No

comment corner — WE'RE PROUD OF YOU stay with it KEEP TRYING BE FAITHFUL you can do it YOU ARE SPECIAL keep going KEEP IT UP GOD LOVES YOU!
Parent or Leader, circle a comment and/or write your own.

Days Completed

Week 46

God's Word—My Truth

Psalm 119 is the longest chapter in the Bible.

SUNDAY
Psalm 119:121-128

May I Serve You?

1. What are the first four words of verse 125?
   _____

2. How many times in these eight verses does the psalmist call himself God's servant? _____

GET STARTED!

Are you willing to be God's servant and to let Him be your master? Yes No
How could you show others that you are God's servant?
_____
_____

MONDAY
Psalm 119:129-136

Unscramble the words. Put the letters from the numbered spaces in their correct spots in the sentence below.

FEAC   [|7| | |]
GIHTL   [|9| | | |]
RODW   [1| |6| |4]
SETRANV [|5| | | | |]
TUMHO   [|2| |8| |]
IEHSN   [| | |3| |]

GOD'S WORD IS [| | | | | | | | |]
               1 2 3 4 5 6 7 8 9

GET STARTED!

Notice that the psalmist asked for God's blessing in verse 135. Would you like to enjoy God's blessings? Yes No
Do you try to obey God's Word every day? Yes No

TUESDAY
Psalm 119:137-144

True or False.

___ God is righteous.

___ God's laws are righteous.

___ God's righteousness is everlasting.

___ God's Word is trustworthy and faithful.

___ God's law is true.

GET STARTED!

Are you always right? Yes No
Is God always right? Yes No
Can you trust God and His commands even when you do not fully understand His plan? Yes No

WEDNESDAY
Psalm 119:145-152

Help Lord!

How did the psalmist cry out? (v. 145) _____
When did he cry out? (v. 147) _____
What did he do at night? (v. 148) _____
He says that his enemies are near, but who else is also near? (v. 151) _____

 The psalmist is in BIG trouble and he needs God's help! Have you ever felt like that? Yes No What should you do when you are stressed out? _____

THURSDAY
Psalm 119:153-160

Solve the puzzle to find today's treasure.

 Will God ever lie to you or try to trick you? Yes No
Write down the name of someone you trust. _____
Who can you trust more, the person you wrote above or God? _____

FRIDAY
Psalm 119:161-168

Complete the sentences by unscrambling the words.

I _____ (jecoier) in your promise. (v. 162)
I _____ (thea) lying and falsehood. (v. 163)
I _____ (evol) your law. (v. 163)
I _____ (sperai) You, God! (v. 164)

 Do you rejoice in God's Word? Yes No
Write out one of your favorite verses from Psalm 119.
_____
_____
_____
_____

SATURDAY
Psalm 119:169-176

Circle the word that you think describes how the psalmist is talking to God.

DEMANDING   HUMBLE

Use the picture code to find out what the word supplication means in verse 170.

 When people came before a king, they were expected to bow their heads and kneel down. Don't you think that the King of kings should have the same respect? Today when you pray, bow your head and kneel down to remind you to be humble before your Almighty God.

107

Week 47

Be a Christian Walkie-Talkie

SUNDAY
Romans 1:1-7

During the life of Christ and the early church, five men were emperors of Rome. A Roman emperor was treated like a god. The Senate could vote to worship an emperor after he died.

Answer the following question about Paul's letter to the church in Rome.

1. How does verse 1 describe Paul?

A _____ of Jesus Christ and an _____

Darken the letters that *do not* belong to reveal how verse 7 describes the people from the church in Rome.

BZZEZZLZZZOZVZZZEZZZD OF GOD AND ZZZZSZZAZIZZZZNZZTZS

Get Started! Write a letter to your pastor or your leader to tell him about when you were saved.

MONDAY
Romans 1:16-17

Find the words in the puzzle.

```
S V G O K F K E T B
W A R O E M N B S E
X G L F S O D R I L
G S M V Y P E P R I
F Z M R A W E G H E
N P E K O T X L C V
Q V Y P F T I G X E
E E O C B A J O A T
P T K J H R P S N H
A S H A M E D J D X
```

ASHAMED BELIEVE (BELIEVETH) CHRIST
EVERYONE GOSPEL POWER SALVATION

Get Started! Make a plan of how you will share Christ with others.

TUESDAY
Romans 1:20-23

Can anyone give an excuse for not knowing that God exists? _____
What did Paul call a person who doesn't believe in God? (v. 22)

_____

CREATION

EVOLUTION

Get Started! Ask your parents, Sunday school teacher, or Olympian leader to explain to you why Christians believe in Creation and not in evolution.

108

WEDNESDAY
Romans 2:8-11

One day, every person will stand before God to answer Him for each of his actions. Circle the answer that fits you.

1. Are you selfish?   Guilty   Not Guilty
2. Are you stubborn?   Guilty   Not Guilty
3. Have you been disobedient this week at home?   Guilty   Not Guilty

 Remember, you do not get to Heaven by being good but by putting your faith in Jesus Christ. However, a person who is a Christian shows his faith by doing good.

THURSDAY
Romans 2:17-24.

The Jews bragged about being special to God because they had the Law. However, the actions of the Jews caused the Gentiles to turn away from God. Would an unsaved person want to become a Christian after watching your life? Circle the actions that show an unsaved person you love God.

Reading your Bible   Lying to your parents   Calling people names   Obeying your teachers

Hitting people   Going to church   Being kind with your words   Praying

 Write a grade for yourself this week.
My Christian walk _____
My Christian talk _____

FRIDAY
Romans 3:4-8

IS IT RIGHT?

Is it right to tell a lie so that you don't get into trouble? _____

Is it right to cheat on a test so you don't get a bad grade? _____

Is it right to pretend to be a Christian even if you're not? _____

Is it right that any one will get to Heaven no matter what he believes? _____

If you have a question about what is right, make sure you check God's Word. He is always right!

SATURDAY
Romans 3:10-18

Write the parts of the body that can be involved in sin in the crossword below.

What is one way you can use your mouth and feet to serve the Lord today?

comment corner WE'RE PROUD OF YOU stay with it KEEP TRYING BE FAITHFUL you can do it YOU ARE SPECIAL keep going KEEP IT UP GOD LOVES YOU!

Days Completed

Parent or Leader, circle a comment and/or write your own.

Week 48

Eternal Life – Free but Not Cheap

Paul often compared sin with slavery. A person who could not pay their bills became a slave until he was able to pay off what he owed.

SUNDAY
Romans 3:22-28

Color in the dotted areas to find out what everyone needs to have in Jesus Christ in order to get to Heaven.

After you finish the puzzle, find and circle this word in your Bible in today's verses.

How many times did you find this word? _____

Jews need it! **Gentiles need it!** **You need it!**

   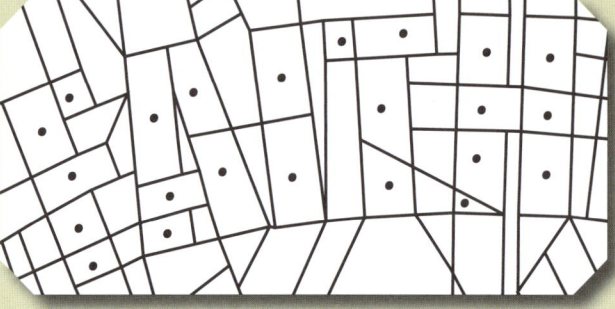

GET STARTED! Have you put your faith in Jesus Christ? If so, share this decision with a friend. If you have not put your faith in Jesus Christ and would like to do that today, talk to a parent or leader.

MONDAY
Romans 4:2-3

Throughout his life, Abraham did many good deeds, but these good deeds are not what got him to Heaven. Fill in the letters below to find out what got Abraham to Heaven (v. 3).

A••R•H••
B•L••V••
G•••

GET STARTED! Do you know someone who thinks that his good works will get him to Heaven? Share with that person what the Bible teaches about going to Heaven.

TUESDAY
Romans 4:16-20

One word in each statement is incorrect. Cross out the incorrect word and write the correct word in the space after the statement.

1. God made Abraham the brother of many nations. _____
2. Abraham was about twenty years old (v. 19) _____
3. Abraham was weak in his faith. _____

Circle the words which tell about you.
I trust God:
- Some of the time
- Most of the time
- All the time
- Never

WEDNESDAY
Romans 5:6-8

Put an X on the line next to each kind of person for whom Jesus died.

 ___ A perfect (righteous) person

 ___ A good person

 ___ A bad (ungodly) person

 Which type of person are you? Jesus loves you so much that He died for you, no matter which type you are.

THURSDAY
Romans 5:14-19

The verses you read today compare Adam and Jesus. Draw a line from the words in the middle to the person it matches.

ADAM

- Sinner
- free gift
- Savior
- death
- eternal life
- obedience
- disobedience
- grace

JESUS

Take the sin test. Is it hard for you to admit it when you sin? Yes No
Do you ask God for forgiveness? Yes No
When you do wrong to another person, do you ask for his forgiveness also? Yes No

FRIDAY
Romans 6:8-12

Write out verse 12 on the lines provided. Color the body that a Christian should want.

_____
_____

SIN   GOD

What sin seems to give you the hardest time (lying, disrespect, laziness, pride...)?
_____

SATURDAY
Romans 6:16-18, 23

Circle the letters that spell the answer to both statements and write it in the spaces.

BEFORE a person gets saved, they are a _____ to SIN.

AFTER a person gets saved, they are a _____ to RIGHTEOUSNESS.

S E L R A V A E N R T

 Memorize Romans 6:23. It is an important verse to know as you talk to others about salvation. Say the verse to your parents.

comment corner

WE'RE PROUD OF YOU · stay with it · KEEP TRYING · BE FAITHFUL · you can do it · YOU ARE SPECIAL · keep going · KEEP IT UP · GOD LOVES YOU!

Days Completed

Parent or Leader, circle a comment and/or write your own.

Week 49 — Make the Mistakes of Yesterday Your Lessons for Today

During this time, about one in every four people was a slave. People became slaves if they were born to parents of slaves, could not pay their debts, or they were captured in battle.

SUNDAY
Romans 7:4-6

Once you are saved, the Holy Spirit lives in you to help you to make good decisions. Find the following words in the puzzle below.

CHRIST
FRUIT
GOD
LAW
SERVE
SPIRIT

```
L G V R I S J B M D I P
A O W L N Z C H R I S T
W D C E V R E S D R D A
S P I R I T I U R F E G
```

Circle the word in dark print that tells about you. Yesterday I made **good** or **bad** decisions. If you circled bad, pray and ask the Lord to forgive you.

MONDAY
Romans 7:14-19

True or False.

_____ The law is spiritual.
_____ I am spiritual.
_____ I want to do good, but instead I do evil.

What should I do?

Finish the sentence.
I will _____ the next time I want to sin.

TUESDAY
Romans 8:5-8

Draw a line from the words on the left to the kind of thinking it describes on the right.

Peace
Sin
Death
Life
Enemy of God

SINFUL NATURE (Carnally Minded)

SPIRITUAL NATURE (Mind set on the Spirit)

Complete the following sentence.
My sinful nature may want to _____ but my spiritual nature says _____.

112

WEDNESDAY
Romans 8:13-17

Unscramble the letters to finish the phrases found in today's passage.

1. (LENRDCIH) _C_ _ _ _ _ _ _ _ _ _ _ of God (v. 16)
2. (RHISE) _H_ _ _ _ _ _ _ of God (v. 17)

The fear of the Lord used in verse 10 means that we should give God the respect He deserves.

Write in your prayer diary the names of your family members who may not be part of God's family. Pray for them today.

THURSDAY
Romans 8:26-28

Fill in the blanks to find out what the Holy Spirit does for every believer.
When does the Holy Spirit help us (v. 26)?
_____
_____

When we, as believers, do not know how to pray, what does the Holy Spirit do for us (v. 26)?
_____
_____

Write out verse 28 and share it with someone today.
_____
_____
_____

FRIDAY
Romans 9:14-16

Everyone deserves God's judgment. Use the clues to help you find the word that describes what God offers to all.

Clue # 1. Write the letter that looks like two mountains together. ____
Clue # 2. Write the letter that comes between D and F. ____
Clue # 3. Write the fourth letter of the place you go to worship God on Sunday. ____
Clue # 4. Write the letter that sounds like the word see. ____
Clue # 5. Write the letter that is next to the last letter in the alphabet. ____

Is every person in your family a Christian? **Yes No** Put the names of unsaved family members on your prayer pages in the front of your Quiet Time and pray for them faithfully to come to know Jesus as their Savior.

SATURDAY
Romans 9:18-21

A piece of pottery becomes what you want it to be. Are you allowing God to make you into what He wants you to be? Unscramble the words which do not allow God to help you. Some of the letters are given.

TBORBUSN	S _ _ BB _ _ N
DSBDETIOEIN	D _ S _ _ _ _ I _ _ T
ELFSSHI	S _ _ F _ _ H
MENA	M _ _ N

Is there a word in the list that describes you? If so, pray and ask God to help you change.

---

comment corner — WE'RE PROUD OF YOU · stay with it · KEEP TRYING · BE FAITHFUL · you can do it · YOU ARE SPECIAL · keep going · KEEP IT UP · GOD LOVES YOU!

Days Completed

Parent or Leader, circle a comment and/or write your own.

Week 50

Israel Rejects but God Restores

The Romans taxed the Jews for many things, even for worshipping in the temple.

SUNDAY
Romans 10:9-13

When Christ died on the cross and rose again three days later, He offered the free gift of salvation to everyone! What does verse 9 say that you need to do to be saved?

C _____ with your mouth

B _____ in your heart

Have you ever asked Jesus to forgive your sins and be your Savior? If so, tell a parent, leader, or friend about it. If you have not asked Jesus to be you Savior, talk to a parent of leader about how you can ask Jesus to forgive your sins.

MONDAY
Romans 10:14-17

During this time people wore sandals. Their feet would get very dirty from walking on dusty or muddy roads. How does verse 15 describe the feet of those who walk around sharing the Gospel? Write each letter on a footprint.

Use your feet to take a Gospel tract to someone who does not know Jesus as their Savior.

TUESDAY
Romans 11:1-4

Elijah felt all alone because he was surrounded by many people who did not worship God. God reminded Elijah that _____ people in Israel still worshipped God. Color in the right number.

7,700

7,000

70,000

Have you ever felt alone like Elijah did? Find a prayer partner at church to share prayer requests with this week.

WEDNESDAY
Romans 11:13-14

Put the names in the correct places. One word is used twice.

The _____ are God's chosen people. However, only a small number accepted _____ as their personal Savior. God chose _____ to preach the Gospel to the _____. Paul willingly shared the Gospel to the _____ but also hoped that Jewish people would accept Christ, too.

CHRIST   JEWS   PAUL   GENTILES

GET STARTED! Don't be discouraged if you tell someone about Jesus, and he doesn't want to accept Him as his personal Savior. Keep praying for that person. Write the name of an unsaved friend you are praying for in the blank. _____

THURSDAY
Romans 11:32-33

Fill in the missing letters to find three characteristics of God found in the verses today.

1. M ☐ ☐ ☐ ☐   (v. 32)
2. W ☐ ☐ ☐ ☐   (v. 33)
3. K ☐ ☐ ☐ ☐   D ☐ ☐   (v. 33)

GET STARTED! God shows mercy to you. Is there someone you need to forgive or ask for forgiveness?

FRIDAY
Romans 12:3-8

As a Christian you received a gift. Not the kind you open, but one that you use to serve others. Fill in the missing words.

What you *don't* want to do with your gift. Think more _____ of yourself than you ought.

What you *do* want to remember. You are part of one _____ of _____.

GET STARTED! Ask your parents or teachers to help you discover your part in the body of Christ.

SATURDAY
Romans 12:17-21

Verse 20 lists some ways to treat your enemies. What is the most important thing that you need to do for your enemy? Use the key to answer this question.

Y	L	E	O	N	U	V	R	M	I	S
1	2	3	4	5	6	7	8	9	10	11

___ ___ ___   ___ ___ ___ ___   ___ ___ ___ ___ ___ ___ ___
2 4 7 3   1 4 6 8   3 5 3 9 10 3 11

GET STARTED! Is someone picking on you? Read verses 17 and 18 again. Write down how you will act when that person annoys you. _____

comment corner
WE'RE PROUD OF YOU   stay with it   KEEP TRYING BE FAITHFUL   you can do it   YOU ARE SPECIAL   keep going   KEEP IT UP   GOD LOVES YOU!

Parent or Leader, circle a comment and/or write your own.

Days Completed

Week 51

Help Wanted

Nero was a cruel Roman emperor who tortured many Christians. When Paul called for obedience to the government, Nero's government was in power. Nero had Paul and Peter executed.

SUNDAY
Romans 13:1-6

Circle the correct answer according to the verses.

Verse 1: Who allows people to be the leaders?
Voters   God

Verse 4: Leaders are put in charge of us
to make us afraid.   for our good.

Verse 5: We are to obey our leaders, not only because we might get punished, but also for our
Conscience   Parents

Verse 6 and 7: Everyone should pay their taxes.
Yes   No

GET STARTED! You have rules everywhere you go: in your home, school, on the playground, etc. Write down two rules that your parents have given you to obey.

_____   _____

MONDAY
Romans 14:1-6

A new Christian may not know very much about the Bible. Circle the statements that would help the new Christian become a stronger Christian.

Read the Bible   Pray   Memorize Bible verses   Lie
Steal   Go to church
Use bad words   Tell someone about Jesus   Cheat

CHRISTIAN IN TRAINING

GET STARTED! What are you doing to become a stronger Christian? Choose one of the items you circled and try it this week.

TUESDAY
Romans 14:13, 19-21

As a Christian your actions should not be a bad example to another Christian. Unscramble the blocks to make a word that tells what a Christian should _not_ be (v.13).

Blocks: I, K, T, N, L, B, U, O

S __ __ M __ __ __ G
B __ __ C __

GET STARTED! Write down one way you can cause another Christian to stumble.

_____

Cross out your answer and replace it with a way to help that Christian instead.

_____

116

WEDNESDAY
Romans 15:2-7

Draw a line from the words to the correct space in which it belongs.

PRESENT **LEARN**

We should ○ our lessons from people who lived in the ○ which encourage us in the ○ and give us ○ for the ○. To do this, we must use the life of ○ as our example.

PAST **FUTURE** **CHRIST** **HOPE**

 Write down two ways you can show respect for God. _____

THURSDAY
Romans 15:17-21

Paul preached the Gospel in cities and countries where the people had not heard about Jesus Christ. On the lines below list missionaries you know and the country (or area) in which they serve. Don't forget to include your Word of Life missionary.

Missionary Name   **Country (or area)**

_____   _____
_____   _____
_____   _____

 Add these missionaries to your prayer journal in the front of your Quiet Time and pray for them today.

FRIDAY
Romans 16:3-5

Paul lists many people who are serving the Lord or have helped Paul in his ministry. Two people mentioned in verses 3 and 4 helped Paul in an important way. What are their names?

P _____ and
A _____
What did they do for Paul? They
_____
_____
_____
their lives for Paul.

 Our anger can stir up anger in others. Love can cause anger and fighting to stop. This week, when you find that someone is angry, try a quiet voice and a loving attitude.

SATURDAY
Romans 16:17-19

True or False.

 Circle the picture of what you should follow.

The Crowd  **The Cross**

____ 1. Some people will cause problems and not follow God's teaching.

____ 2. Hang around these disobedient people and listen to them.

____ 3. These kinds of people are trying to deceive others.

____ 4. Verse 19 says that the people were obedient.

comment corner — WE'RE PROUD OF YOU · stay with it · KEEP TRYING BE FAITHFUL · you can do it · YOU ARE SPECIAL · keep going · KEEP IT UP · GOD LOVES YOU!

Parent or Leader, circle a comment and/or write your own.

Days Completed

Week 52
Hosea's Heart Healthy News

What is your favorite dessert? The Israelites liked raisin cakes. They even used them as offerings to idols when they strayed away from God.

SUNDAY
Hosea 4:1-2

Circle the three things God says are missing from the Israelite's lives. (v.1) Put X's over the five sins happening throughout Israel. (v.2)

> Murder (killing)　love　money　stealing　faithfulness
> food　truth　lying (deception)
> adultery　knowledge of God　mercy　swearing (cursing)

GET STARTED! Are any one of the items you circled missing from your life? Confess it to God and ask Him to change your heart.

MONDAY
Hosea 4:16-17

The Israelites kept making the same mistakes. Avoid the traps in the maze to show the Israelites the way out.

selfishness

laziness

anger

lying

GET STARTED! Is there a sin (lying, losing your temper, being lazy,...) that you have trouble overcoming? **Yes   No** Ask for God's help. Then go to your parents and ask for their help.

TUESDAY
Hosea 6:1-3

Circle the correct words to finish the statements.

1. Come, let us _____ the Lord.
   run from   return to

2. God has torn us but He will _____ us.
   heal   reward

3. God will revive us in _____ days.
   two   three

4. God will raise us up (restore us) in _____ days.
   two   three

5. God will come to us like _____.
   rain   thunder

GET STARTED! Yesterday, you confessed a sin to God. Have you avoided that sin today? **Yes   No** Stop right now and pray, asking God to help you avoid the sin and to help you seek Him.

118

WEDNESDAY
Hosea 10: 12

Verse 12 has a message for the Israelites that is true for you. Fill in the missing vowels.

For it is time to seek the Lord

Finish the sentence.
I will seek God today by_____.

THURSDAY
Hosea 11:1-9

Complete the crossword puzzle with words that show God's love.

ACROSS
1. verse 3: They did not know it was God who ___ them.
4. verse 1: When Israel was a child (youth) God ___ him.
5. verse 4a: God led them with bands (ties) of ___.

DOWN
2. verse 9a: God will not execute (carry out) His fierce ___.
3. verse 9b: God is God, not man. He is the ___ ___.

God loves you and wants you to love others. Do something special for someone in your home today to show him or her God's love.

FRIDAY
Hosea 13:4-9

Write in your own words what God did for Israel from verses 4-6.
_____
_____

Circle the correct answer:

During the drought, God made Israel _____

empty   filled

Who will help Israel? (v.9)
_____

Share a prayer request with a friend. Be sure to pray for each other every day.

SATURDAY
Hosea 14:4-9

Follow the lines to put the bubble letters in place to see what the Israelites learned.

"The ways of the Lord are right, and we should walk in them."

How faithful have you been this week? Write the number of days you completed your Quiet Time in the box below.

comment corner WE'RE PROUD OF YOU stay with it KEEP TRYING BE FAITHFUL you can do it YOU ARE SPECIAL keep going KEEP IT UP GOD LOVES YOU! Days Completed

Parent or Leader, circle a comment and/or write your own.

To Word of Life Club Members

To allow you to see which books of the Bible you will be covering in this year's Quiet Time please refer to the weekly passages listed below. These are the same passages used in all Word of Life Quiet Times. And if you would like to listen to the daily Quiet Time radio broadcasts the corresponding dates are listed as well.

week 1	Aug 29 – Sep 4	Psalms 104:1-105:45
week 2	Sep 5 – Sep 11	Psalms 106:1-108:13
week 3	Sep 12 – Sep 18	Psalms 109:1-113:9
week 4	Sep 19 – Sep 25	2 Corinthians 1:1-4:18
week 5	Sep 26 – Oct 2	2 Corinthians 5:1-8:24
week 6	Oct 3 – Oct 9	2 Corinthians 9:1-13:14
week 7	Oct 10 – Oct 16	1 Samuel 1:1-9:27
week 8	Oct 17 – Oct 23	1 Samuel 10:1-17:16
week 9	Oct 24 – Oct 30	1 Samuel 17:17-20:42
week 10	Oct 31 – Nov 6	2 Samuel 5:1-23:7
week 11	Nov 7 – Nov 13	James 1:1-3:10
week 12	Nov 14 – Nov 20	James 3:11-5:20
week 13	Nov 21 – Nov 27	Proverbs 21:1-23:25
week 14	Nov 28 – Dec 4	Proverbs 23:26-25:28
week 15	Dec 5 – Dec 11	1 Peter 1:1-3:7
week 16	Dec 12 – Dec 18	1 Peter 3:8-5:14
week 17	Dec 19 – Dec 25	Luke 1:1-2:14
week 18	Dec 26 – Jan 1	Luke 2:15-4:15
week 19	Jan 2 – Jan 8	Luke 4:16-6:26
week 20	Jan 9 – Jan 15	Luke 6:27-8:15
week 21	Jan 16 – Jan 22	Luke 8:16-9:50
week 22	Jan 23 – Jan 29	Luke 9:51-11:28
week 23	Jan 30 – Feb 5	Luke 11:29-13:9
week 24	Feb 6 – Feb 12	Luke 13:10-15:32
week 25	Feb 13 – Feb 19	Luke 16:1-18:43
week 26	Feb 20 – Feb 26	Luke 19:1-21:4
week 27	Feb 27 – Mar 5	Luke 21:5-23:12
week 28	Mar 6 – Mar 12	Luke 23:13-24:53
week 29	Mar 13 – Mar 19	Ezekiel 1:1-11:25
week 30	Mar 20 – Mar 26	Ezekiel 12:17-20:16
week 31	Mar 27 – Apr 2	Ezekiel 20:17-33:20
week 32	Apr 3 – Apr 9	Ezekiel 33:21-37:14
week 33	Apr 10 – Apr 16	Ezekiel 37:15-47:12
week 34	Apr 17 – Apr 23	Philippians 1:1-2:23
week 35	Apr 24 – Apr 30	Philippians 2:24-4:23
week 36	May 1 – May 7	Isaiah 1:1-9:7
week 37	May 8 – May 14	Isaiah 10:16-26:21
week 38	May 15 – May 21	Isaiah 28:5-35:10
week 39	May 22 – May 28	Isaiah 40:1-44:24
week 40	May 29 – June 4	Isaiah 45:5-49:26
week 41	Jun 5 – Jun 11	Isaiah 50:1-57:21
week 42	Jun 12 – Jun 18	Isaiah 58:1-66:24
week 43	Jun 19 – Jun 25	Psalms 114:1-119:8
week 44	Jun 26 – Jul 2	Psalms 119:9-119:64
week 45	Jul 3 – Jul 9	Psalms 119:65-119:120
week 46	Jul 10 – Jul 16	Psalms 119:121-119:176
week 47	Jul 17 – Jul 23	Romans 1:1-3:20
week 48	Jul 24 – Jul 30	Romans 3:21-6:23
week 49	Jul 31 – Aug 6	Romans 7:1-9:33
week 50	Aug 7 – Aug 13	Romans 10:1-12:21
week 51	Aug 14 – Aug 20	Romans 13:1-16:27
week 52	Aug 21 – Aug 27	Hosea 3:4-14:19